STOP NOW!

Before opening this book, I (the author), would request of you (the reader) to do yourself, God and me a very important favor.

PRAY!

Pray a little prayer every time you open this book to partake. Ask God, by His Holy Spirit, to speak to your heart and reveal all of what He has to say to you in your reading.

As the author, I know that the Logos (written Word), can never become Rhema (living Word), unless God is involved and therefore giving you revelation important for your application of this work in your life.

Revelation-The divine or supernatural disclosure to humans of something relating to human existence or the world.

This book can change your life If you allow God, by His Holy Spirit, to intervene in your reading it!

God Bless your reading.

Don Brown

D1518667

ISBN: 9798650868217
Cover Design: Peter Mealy
Cover Photography: Mats Jerndal, Oddbox Media Inc.
*Unless otherwise noted all Scripture quotations are taken
from:
The New King James Version.
1982 by Thomas Nelson Inc.
Used by permission. All rights reserved.
Message Bible. 2002 **by** Eugene H. Peterson. Used by
permission.
All rights reserved.

Contact:
Don Brown (540) 455-4921
@Facebook- Don Brown Media
donbrownmusic.com
donbrownrun2u@yahoo.com

Acknowledgements

First and foremost, I would like to thank my Lord and Savior Jesus Christ, and The Holy Spirit that He sent to live in me for so many years. His presence alone inspired me to write my daily posts, and enabled me to compile them into *Morning Meditations*. I realize I am nothing without the presence of God in my life and can do nothing worthwhile without His blessings.

For the many inspirational sermons and informative bible studies, I would like to thank posthumously, Apostle John Meares of Evangel Temple(Church), and Apostle Patricia Tyous of Greater Holy Lighthouse of Prayer. In my walk in the Kingdom of God these two leaders have been the ultimate in teachers. Dare I not mention Bishop Don Meares, one of the most dynamic teachers of the bible I have sat under at Evangel Temple who taught me so much. Lastly, but certainly not least, I cannot fail to mention Apostle Kevin Mihlfeld of Strong Tower Ministries. His way of breaking down the scripture often left me with my mouth hanging open in awe! All of these people were truly God's Generals in my life, and allowed themselves to be used in shaping this Kingdom kid.

After God and His Generals that shaped my understanding of the Word, I must give credit to Peter Mealy. When it came to putting my writings into book form, and submitting my work to the publisher, my friend has been there for me in a major way. I thank God for Peter's friendship. He truly let the Lord use Him and I am forever grateful

Preface

For a quick reference point to what I believe is the most important part of this book, see The Roman Road to Salvation on pages 61-65.

.

This book is a compilation of inspirational posts made on a very popular social network. I was inspired to write them by the Holy Spirit as a source of inspiration for the troubled, unchurched, confused and misled. People like myself who had been erroneously taught the Bible for years in churches that teach a partial gospel.

I have a certain disdain for "preachers" that week after week preach a veiled gospel. "Preachers" that leave their congregants helpless, malnourished and dependent on them for any and all of their knowledge of the Word of God. I believe that folks need to know certain foundational principles of the Word and how to use the Word as a guidebook, roadmap or book of instructions on life. I believe that if these same folks can't get the truth anywhere else, then why not the social media outlets.

I have a heart for people, who like me, have struggled with drug abuse, rejection, incarceration, loneliness, homelessness, child abuse, verbal and physical abuse. My writings are often laced with my testimony, sermons that inspired me and thoughtful quotes from people that have been influential in my life.

The posts contained in this book were a labor of love and obedience. Obedience because it was not my original intent to sit down each morning, five days a week and write them. I joined social media to advertise for my band functions and to get people to support my shows since that was the only way that I got paid. I then somehow got caught up in the gossip I saw on the pages and began participating, as well as using the pages to flirt. It seemed like a great way to meet members of the opposite sex and possibly find a mate. One day the Holy Spirit spoke to my heart and said "if you are going to talk or write on these pages you must talk about Me". Having been acutely associated with the consequences of disobedience and aware of the many stripes of chastisement that come from a God Who I know loves me dearly, I decided to write about the God of my salvation, sharing what thus said the Lord to me.

Writing these posts daily was not easy. Daily I rose early to leaf through the bible, listen to televangelists or review notes from church sermons. I did this until something jumped out from the pages or a word was spoken, that ministered to me deeply inspiring me to share. Initially I would share whatever the Lord was dealing with me about. To my surprise others would chime in, thanking me for sharing, as they were going through similar struggles.

Many mornings I would have rather slept in until time to go to work. Many other mornings I felt empty with nothing to offer after slipping in my personal walk the night before. Guilt would leave me feeling unworthy to share anything with anybody. I myself felt in need of exhortation. On many of these mornings the Holy Spirit would prompt me to just put my hands on the keyboard and let Him do the writing.
Also on these very mornings often I have had to go back and read what was written more than once. I've been awe-inspired by the power in those posts that helped me more than anybody else, or so I thought.

Comments have been made by people reading the daily posts. Comments such as "I must have been listening to their prayers", or "how could I have spied on them in their bedrooms the night before". My only correct reply was, "surely I wasn't there but the Holy Spirit is omnipresent".

Too numerous were the times when I have been discouraged.Thinking no one was listening, often I made decisions to quit these writings. Whenever this occurred God would place someone outside of my door, eager to share how they read my posts, and were helped by them. These testimonials I took as hearing from God, causing me to repent and get back to writing.

What you are about to read are portions of what has equaled over four years of morning inspirations. My prayer is that they inspire you to achieve great things for the Kingdom of God. Lead others to the cross of Jesus Christ, and be a better soldier in the Kingdom.

May God bless your reading and empower you to be a blessing.

***

Good morning Fam. "To them God willed to make known what are the riches of the glory of this mystery among the Gentiles: which is Christ in YOU the Hope of Glory."

Colossians 1:27

Glory to God! He wants to use you who have accepted Christ to make known the mysteries of God to an unsaved world. Because in YOU lies the HOPE of GLORY.

I want to share with you some good news to start your week. IT'S IN YOU.!!! Fam. The scripture we opened with comes from Colossians. It speaks of a truth often overlooked by the "church". It says that IN YOU lies the hope of glory.

II Corinthians 4:7 goes a step further to say "But we have this treasure in earthen vessels, that the excellence of the power may be of God and not of us."

If you have accepted Christ and are filled with His Spirit, you have in you all that the world needs, seeks, and has gone everywhere else to find the answers to. Think about it! People seek out horoscopes, psychiatrists, Dr.Phil and Oprah to find out the answers to life. When IN YOU lies the Hope Of Glory. Often we have not realized all that God has deposited in us when He gave us His Holy Spirit, Whom He promised will bring us into ALL truth. Coupled with the study of Gods' Word, The Holy Spirit in You is all the truth needed for the world today.

Let's get busy! IT'S IN YOU and the world is hungry for what You have.

I'm jus sayin...Luv me.

***

Good morning Fam.. "For you did not receive the spirit of bondage again to fear, but you received the Spirit of adoption by whom we cry out, "Abba,Father." Rom.8:15.

We cry out daddy, daddy!! God ain't some big bad dude, sitting on a throne somewhere waiting for us to make a mistake so that He can bust us upside the head with a spiritual baseball bat."

"The Spirit Himself bears witness with our spirit that we are children of God". Romans 8:16

I'm jus sayin…...Luv me

***

God morning Fam.."Be diligent to present yourself approved to God, a worker who does not need to be ashamed, rightly dividing the word of truth." 2 Timothy 2:15

"All scripture is given by inspiration of God, and is profitable for doctrine, for reproof, for correction, for instruction in righteousness, that the man (or woman) of God may be complete, thoroughly equipped for every good work". 2 Timothy 3:16-17

Fam. you've got to know the Word for yourself if you want to get the benefits associated with it. What your pastor knows won't prosper you. What you're mom and dad knows will not help you receive your way of escape when the enemy whispers in your ear something that is contrary to the Word.

"For the time will come when they will not endure sound doctrine, but according to their own desires, because they have itching ears, they will heap up for themselves teachers; and they will turn their ears away from the truth, and be turned aside to fables". II Tim.4:3-5

Jim Jones, David Koresh, and many others have led people who had good intentions down a path to self-destruction, only because they did not know the Word for themselves. Their followers, no doubt in my mind, were folks who loved the Lord, but they trusted a man to bring them the truth, and did not "study to show themselves approved".

We have those same options today. We are given the opportunity to either study the Word for ourselves or trust that someone else is telling us what thus says the Lord. There is no power like the power of a group of folk who know the Word for themselves. People who are standing on the infallible Word and receiving the promises of God for themselves. These people cannot be easily led down a path of destruction.

Know the Word for yourself Fam., and experience the freedom that comes with it.

I'm jus sayin...Luv me.

***

Good morning Fam.. Running late for work, oversleeping and it felt good. Know this, whatever you're going through, God is able! He will carry you through. If you just cast your cares on Him and leave them there, not doubting. A double minded man receives nothing from God.

I'm jus sayin...Luv me.

***

TGIF Fam., God morning to you one and all. Psalm 45:1 "My heart is overflowing with a good theme; I recite my composition concerning the King; My tongue is the pen of a ready writer."

As we finish another work week Fam, my prayer is that we get "IT"! The IT that I'm speaking about is your ability to speak life into your life. You have been created to worship God and take dominion in the earth by using our tongue as a creative force for positive change. When we speak the Word as opposed to our current reality, we unleash God to do His good will in our lives and the lives of those around us.

The Word of God is broken down into two parts defined as Logos (written Word) and Rhema (living Word). Many times I have asked you to get to know the Word for yourself. Then and only then you can speak it and use it's creative powers to speak to your issues of life. For the Word to become Rhema, or life, to us individually we must take the time to absorb it into our spirits by studying it for ourselves.

Psalm 119:11 "Your Word have I hidden in my heart that I might not sin against You."

Fam we've got to hide this Word in our hearts. So that no devil can take away our ability to use it in due season as situations arise.

Life happens, and if we have His Word hidden in our hearts we can use our God-given authority to take dominion in the earth. By speaking what God says, instead of what our current reality shows us, we can be agents of positive change affecting folks in a Godly way.

As every week, I will ask, no beg you to find a group of believers who rightfully divide the Word to join with, offering some corporate praise to God. If you need suggestions on where to do this, hit my inbox. God bless you! Go, and be a blessing to someone.

I'm jus sayin...Luv me.

***

IF YOU CAN'T HANDLE THE TRASH IN MY LIFE, DON'T THINK YOU'RE GONNA BE WITH ME WHEN THE TREASURE MANIFESTS.

There is a treasure in each of us, but many want to throw us away because of the trash they see. Jesus died to pay for it all, our trash, and the treasure He wants to bring forth. We all need to love the trash out of people. Then and only then, we will see the treasure manifested.

God Monday to you Fam.. Matthew 13:44 "Again, the kingdom of heaven is like treasure hidden in a field, which a man found and hid; and for joy over it he goes and sells all that he has and buys that field."

Our lives represent the field. When Jesus died on the cross to pay for us, He paid for all that we are and all that we will be. It is no surprise to Jesus, that we are jacked-up and ALL of us still have flaws. Jesus payed for us anyway, so that when we come to Him He can change us into His image and bring forth the true treasure in us. We, the church, have been accused and rightfully so, of judging and turning our noses up to folks still struggling. We have looked down on people instead of investing in them to bring them along with us on a journey to where God wants to take us all.

Kingdom living, with kingdom mindsets, living above and not below, being first and not last, overflowing with more. "Thy kingdom come thy will be done, in earth as it is in heaven". How many times have we recited this verse? Yet some of us cannot fathom living the Kingdom life here on earth, we have been fooled into believing only for that pie in the sky in the great bye and bye. Every one of God's creations have deposited in them a treasure that if allowed will manifest, that if nurtured will come out, that if worked with will shine forth like the morning sun. Sadly many of us have forgotten where we come from. When we see someone struggling, instead of embracing them, we judge and shun them, never seeing them as Jesus sees us all. God forbid. To get to the treasure, we've got to invest in the field, buying all of the junk to harvest a treasure. That's what Jesus did for you.

I'm jus sayin…..Luv me.

***

 God morning Fam.. "Let God arise and His enemies be scattered." Psalm 68:1.

When I first got saved, we sang this song "Let God Arise". It didn't occur to me then, the power in the message of this song. How do we let God arise so that our enemies will scatter?

He must arise by our giving of praise and our worship. The bible clearly says, "God inhabits the praises of His people". His very presence is commanded by the heartfelt, sincere praise from our lips. God is not a man that He should lie. We have to have faith in His Word to perform that which it was sent to accomplish. We must speak The Word to our situations expecting positive results. We have that right!

We can be going through a literal hell on earth, and in a position where the enemy is having his way with everybody around us. It's when we have the faith to praise God with our lips that His enemies will scatter. God's enemies cannot stand in His presence. When we, in obedience, saturate the atmosphere with our praise we create a highway that allows heaven to come to earth. "Thy Kingdom come, thy will be done, on earth as it is in heaven".

God wants us to rest in Him and believe that He not only has our back, but if we are in good/right standing, He leads the way.

Don't get it twisted disobedience and willfully not obeying His will causes us to relinquish our rights to His protection. It has always been in those times that GRACE has covered me, as I just couldn't understand how He still cared enough for me to look out when I didn't even deserve a look..

Fam stop the struggle and praise your way into His presence, so that your enemies will scatter.

I'm jus sayin...Luv me.

***

God Morning Fam.. "And they overcame him (the accuser) by the blood of the Lamb and by the word of their testimony, and they did not love their lives to the death". Revelations 12:11

Fam., this morning I need to share a bit of testimony, as our anointing is in our testimony. Lately the accuser has been trying to push me off of my square, by testing my resolve to trust God.

Yeah, the enemy is using a pawn in his effort to push me off my square. I've heard that dude is gonna beat me up. LOL (laugh out loud) I think this is funny as I am only two inches and a prayer removed from thuggery. I have a bunch of pent-up aggression that I would like to release on someone and I admit I've already envisioned a plan of attack. This would please the devil and my flesh would welcome a good fight, but would it glorify God? I've written that it is not the person offending you who is to blame, it is the spirit using them.

Our battle is not with flesh and blood, but with spiritual wickedness in high places. Ephesians 6:12 (NKJV) **"For we do not wrestle against flesh and blood, but against principalities, against powers, against the rulers of the darkness of this age, against spiritual *hosts* of wickedness in the heavenly *places."***

I've also written about pride. How God hates pride and how pride goes before a fall. Pride is what motivates us to stand up for ourselves and use natural tools (fists) to fight spiritual battles. Pride tells us that we have every right to go find our offender and whip the snot out of them. What then does that say about my confession of faith? What about my testimony?

Today I choose to do things in a way that God would receive glory from it and get the victory. If dude comes around I will hold my peace, however I don't know if I have arrived at the place where I can turn the other cheek. Therefore pray for me Fam.. I ain't tryna (trying to) need bail 4real.!!!! lol

I'm jus sayin...Luv me.

***

Good morning Fam. "If My people who are called by My name will humble themselves, and pray and seek my face, and turn from their wicked ways, then I will hear from heaven, and will forgive their sin and heal their land." II Chronicles 7:14

Fam. we are in perilous times. If you look around with your spiritual eyes, you will notice that the world is heading to hell in a handbasket. Hell in a handbasket (that's an old folks term), as funny as that sounds, it's serious. It is more obvious than ever that we as a people need to humble ourselves, pray, and seek God's face. Then and only then will we hear from heaven and be forgiven. In addition, our place of habitation will be healed.

We have come to a place where people are almost afraid to touch one another. Texting has replaced calling, and we are literally a "no touch generation". "Can't touch this", as M.C. Hammer would say. I have seen folks in the same room texting each other rather than carrying on a conversation. What's that about?

Fam we have got to get back to caring and sharing. Giving special attention to those who are less fortunate. Loving like Jesus loved. Christians(Christlike people) must be ready to get our hands a little soiled. Reaching out with the love of Jesus, getting down and dirty loving on people.

I ask you today when was the last time you helped someone who was homeless? Do you know where to go to do that? Jesus said when you help "the least of these my little ones", you are helping Him. Many will be told on the day of judgement that they did not minister to Jesus, by ministering to folks in need, "the least of these".

I'm saying today, we ought to be about the Fathers business and not so stuck on ourselves. The cross is pointed in two directions, vertical pointing to God and horizontal reaching out to men.

I'm jus sayin...Luv me.

***

Good morning and TGIF Fam… The weekend is once again upon us. Time for many of us to catch up on the things we can't get done during the work week. I would like to leave you this week with a thought from Galatians chapter 6.

"Do not be deceived, God is not mocked; for whatever a man sows, that he will also reap. For he who sows to his flesh will of the flesh reap corruption, but he who sows to the Spirit will of the Spirit reap everlasting life."

Fam. simply put, you reap what you sow. Therefore, I would encourage all, to sow some love this weekend. Sow some forgiveness. Sow some of that paycheck into a ministry that is flourishing in the Word. Sow some kindness into the lives of someone you don't even know. Sow some positive encouragement into the lives of our youth. When you do these things expect, and watch for your harvest to come in.

As every week at this time. I will leave you asking, no begging you to find a body of believers that rightfully divide the Word. Join with them in offering God some corporate praise.
SOW SOME LOVE!!!

I'm jus sayin...Luv me.

***

Good morning Fam.. In the midst of all the birthday wishes from yesterday. I think some of us missed one of the most profound "now words" ever posted. For this reason I will repost and I pray it helps someone.

Proverbs 18:21 "Death and life are in the power of the tongue, And those who love it will eat its fruit."

Fam, especially parents, we have to be careful what we speak into our lives and the lives of those we come into contact with. Our words have a creative force that can build up or tear down.

Growing up, throughout elementary school I was an honor roll student. Yet at home all I heard was, "you ain't got no common sense", "you're never going to be nothing", and other statements that made me feel like I was not good enough. I thought my name was stupid mutha_____ .

Robbed of my self-esteem I had no self worth. Therefore I sought to be important by hustling the streets. I thought, no one has to do anything for me, I will do for myself. If I get money people will know how smart I am, I surmised. I also skipped school many days to get high, since my academic achievements from elementary school were not so important. This is what I was led to believe by the statements I heard at home. I would skip thirty days a semester from a class and still come out with a C. What if I hadn't skipped?

When time came to go to college I had neglected High School so badly my mom would not even sign the papers. Little did I know that this was in God's plan.

I escaped my little hometown and made it to Egypt (Washington D.C.).

In Washington after searching for the truth trying Sun Young Moon and the Muslim mosque, I came to know Jesus as my personal Savior. For the first time I was told that I was special.

I achieved much and rose quickly in the retail shoe business world. I was made a manager of a store at age eighteen and wore a suit and tie to work daily. With that position I finally realized my name was Mr. Don Brown. In God's and the world's eyes I was important. I was somebody, not stupid, not a failure, or some of the other things I was labeled as, as a child.

Parents, the things you say to your children now are shaping his or her future. When you tell them positive things it nurtures their self esteem, builds them up and gives them confidence. Quite the opposite happens when you speak negativity, it tears them down and destroys any confidence they may have. Intentional or not, your words count and shape your children's perceptions of themselves. There is absolute power in your words, negative or positive.

I've said it before and I'll say it again, "Watch Yo Mouth".

Im jus sayin...Luv me.

***

"Take me back, take me back Dear Lord. To the place, where I first received you. Take me back, take me back Dear Lord, where I first believed". This was a very popular song in the early contemporary gospel music genre, written by a pioneer of the sound, Andre Crouch.

Does anybody remember that place, when you first received, believed, invited, trusted, LOVED, and accepted Christ into your heart?

Good morn. Fam.. "and you have persevered and have patience, and have labored for My names' sake and have not become weary. Nevertheless I have this against you, that you have left your first love. Remember therefore from where you have fallen; repent and do the first works". Revelations 2:4-5

I have been feeling a pull in my spirit lately, a prompting to return to that place I was in when I first met the Lord. Is there anyone who can relate this morning?

I'm talking about that place where I was so in love with my new found relationship with Christ. I studied His Word fervently, and fasted for two to six days a week because I wanted more of Him and less of me. I trusted the Word totally and when prompted to lay hands on the sick, I did because I was to dumb to believe anything other than The Word. People were being healed and set free, only because I was able to trust without reserve.

If you've ever been in love, I'm sure you remember when you first met and opened up the lines of communication with her or him. You would talk on the phone all night, and upon hanging up would be tempted to call back. You thought about that person incessantly and all you wanted with every fiber in you, was to be with that person or at the least hear their voice.

Then you became familiar. To be satisfied didn't take so much conversation. You could spend more and more time away from that person without longing for them. It was just a natural progression.

God is saying in the verses from Revelations above, that this is how many of us have treated our relationship with Him. God's desire is for us to fall in love all over again and treat Him like we did when we first received Him. OH SO IN LOVE, and He uses a word that is not so popular in the church today, REPENT(to have a godly sorrow for and turn completely away from your wrong).

I know this is a Word for me, how about you?

I'm jus sayin...Luv me.

***

Good morning Fam.. "This Book of the Law shall not depart from your mouth, but you shall meditate in it day and night, that you may observe to do according to all that is written in it. For then you will make your way prosperous, and then you will have good success. Have I not commanded you? Be strong and of good courage; do not be afraid, nor be dismayed, for the Lord your God is with you wherever you go". Joshua 1:8-9

It's the meditating on the Word that allows It to become more than LOGOS (written words). We all should have a strong desire for the Word to become Rhema (living, alive and active). It is then and only then, that it will accomplish all that it is sent to do. Transforming our lives into the thing that God wants it to become. A vessel of hope, love, and an agent of and from Heaven.

I'm jus sayin...Luv me.

***

1 John 4:7-8 "Beloved, let us love one another, for love is of God; and everyone who loves is born of God and knows God. He who does not love, does not know God, for God is love".
Fam we need to check our love, examine ourselves, and line up our actions against the Word. Periodically we ought to ask the Holy Spirit to show us if we are loving as God loves us. It's easy to say you love someone at church, during the Pastor induced "love sessions". When the pastor commands you to go to your brother and tell them you love them, that's easy as we are only being obedient to the Pastor. To know if we really love we have to line our own love up against the Word of God.

One of my favorite books of the Bible is I Corinthians 13. By studying this book I found out that my love game was suffering.

Example: Verse 4 "Love suffers long and is kind; love does not envy; love does not parade itself, is not puffed up".

When was the last time we truly suffered anything for the sake of loving someone else? Oh no that isn't convenient and maybe God didn't mean it that way, we surmise. When our love costs us something we often shut that one out, "it's got to be easy or I ain't doing it". Wow! Is that truly God's kind of love? He loves us so much that He not only puts up with our shortcomings, He chose to give His life knowing about them before they were.

The rest of this chapter in I Corinthians really gets to the meat of God's definition of love. I pray that we all would study it for ourselves and get our love game up, it's imperative if we want to please a loving God.

Let us not love in word only, but let us love with our deeds, many will be shocked one day when Jesus Himself tells us that we never loved Him, because we did not do for the "least of these, His little ones". That's a word for another day. Have a blessed day!

I'm jus sayin...Luv me.

***

Good morning Fam..Rom.12:9-13 "Let love be without hypocrisy. Abhor what is evil. Cling to what is good. Be kindly affectionate to one another with brotherly love, in honor giving preference to one another; not lagging in diligence, fervent in spirit, serving the Lord; rejoicing in hope, patient in tribulation, continuing steadfastly in prayer; distributing to the needs of the saints, given to hospitality."

Fam lately the Lord has had me sharing about love. Love is of God and if we claim Him, it is our duty to raise our love to His level. I know sometimes it's hard. People will pluck your nerves, wound you, and make false accusations against you. Others will take your kindness for weakness and trample on your feelings while taking advantage of you. Nevertheless we who claim Jesus have to lick our wounds and love as he loved.

His kind of love looked into the face of a people who called for His execution after He had done nothing but love them, heal them, and bring heaven to their earthly existence. The way Jesus was treated was enough for many of us to declare. "I'm done with those folks, they no longer exist", and throw them away for life. Most of us would have done just that. BUT GOD being who He is, chose to stay on that rugged cross where he would die a horrible death, and He forgave all who would believe.

I give this analogy whenever I am dealing with someone holding onto unforgiveness from past hurts from people. Today I ask you. Has that person who has done you wrong, done more to you than they did to Jesus? Well, you must forgive and love even moreso.

Grandma used to say "sometimes you've got to feed people with a long handled spoon". What she was saying was, we still got to feed them. Romans 12:13"distributing to the needs of the saints". It's still gotta be done.

I'm jus sayin...Luv me.

***

Good morning Fam, nothing I have tried to post has worked this morning, evidently not God's will. But I will once again try the prayer.

Dear Lord I come to You on this day with a heart of thanksgiving. Thanking You for all of my SM Fam. Thanking You for Your plan of salvation and most of all Your Son Jesus Christ who was sent to us as a payment for our sins. Lord grant us all a new start on this day and create in us a clean heart, a heart that would be compassionate, loving and caring as You are. Help us all to see past our differences for the greater glory of what You have for us individually and collectively. Help us to hunger and thirst after righteousness and renew a right Spirit in us.

Lord as I come to You, I ask for a blood covering over Your people and especially our leaders in the Body of Christ. Make all crooked paths straight. Give us the wisdom to know the difference between Your voice and the voice of the deceiver. I come against all forces of the enemy to divide the body of Christ and cause us to war amongst ourselves. Let us all focus on the path You have placed us on and not worry about others, but trust that You have it all under control.

I pray now all these things, In the precious name of Jesus, and by faith I call them done.

***

God morning Fam. James 4:10 "Humble yourselves in the sight of the Lord, and He will lift you up. Do not speak evil of one another, brethren. He who speaks evil of a brother and judges a brother, speaks evil of the law and judges the law. But if you judge the law, you are not a doer of the law but a judge. There is

one Lawgiver, who is able to save and to destroy. Who are you to judge another?"
Religion accuses and condemns. Relationship loves and restores. Religion points out all faults and is sure to expose them to the world. Relationship sees the fault, goes to the one at fault privately and attempts to correct in love. Religion broadcasts others sins and seeks to push it's self righteous agenda down everyone's throat, while forgetting that they were born in sin and shaped in iniquity. Relationship attempts to cover a brother in love, never forgetting that they too needed a cover one day and God sent someone for them.

Fam I have always said that I hate the religious and cling to the relational. You yourselves watch folks in the coming weeks, months and see which side you are on Religious, or Relational.

I'm jus sayin...Luv me.

***

"Now therefore, listen to me my children, For blessed are those who keep my ways. Hear instruction and be wise, And do not disdain it. Blessed is the man who listens to me, Watching daily at my gates, waiting at the posts of my doors. For whoever find me finds life, And obtains favor from the Lord; But he who sins against me wrongs his own soul; All those who hate me love death".

Good morn. Fam above you have read Proverbs 8:32-36. Proverbs is considered by many as a book full of the wisdom a father would pass on to his son. This book of the bible was written by Solomon, David's son. Solomon who is known for receiving wisdom unlike any other before him, simply because he had the chance to ask for anything of God. Solomon asked God for nothing but wisdom.

That seemed like a smart thing to do, for when Solomon asked for wisdom he received riches also.

Some of us will never get riches, because we don't have the wisdom not to kill ourselves with the riches, once they are released. I don't know about you, but I believe and have confessed that this is partly why I myself am not rich yet. God will never put more on you than you can bear.

I'm jus sayin...Luv me.

***

God morning Fam and TGIF once again. Lately I have been stuck in Proverbs and I truly ain't mad about it. In the book of Proverbs God speaks instructions on life. Today in the comment boxes I'll post a few proverbs that speak to me and I pray that they help you.
"A fool vents all his feelings, But a wise man holds them back". Proverbs 29:11

"The rod and rebuke give wisdom, But a child left to himself brings shame to his mother." Proverbs 29:15
"Do you see a man hasty in his words? There is more hope for a fool than for him." Proverbs 29:20

"A mans pride will bring him low, But the humble in spirit will retain honor." Proverbs 29:23

"The discretion of a man makes him slow to anger, and it is his glory to overlook a transgression."Proverbs 19:11

" He who has knowledge spares his words, And a man of understanding is of a calm spirit. Even a fool is counted wise when he holds his peace; when he shuts his lips, he is considered perceptive." Proverbs 17:27-28

I'm jus sayin...Luv me.

***

God morning Fam. This is the day that the Lord has made, I will rejoice and be glad in it. You can talk about rainy Monday, Monday being a bad day, etcetera, but I will thank God for this day. It is the first day of the rest of my life, therefore I will bless it with my lips and not curse it with the same lips that were meant to pour forth praise.

Recently I was given a word, that the Lord wants me to spend more time in His Word. I received that word with gladness as I believe that He is taking me to new heights in Him and is wanting to prepare me for the journey. God is in fact moving in the lives of His people and is doing the miraculous so that it cannot be denied that it was God who did it. Many will be drawn to Him through His mighty acts.

I have always said that as I receive I will pass what I receive on to you. Therefore I am sharing today, God wants us all to spend more time in His Word.

Psalm 119:11"Thy Word have I hidden in my heart that I might not sin against thee".

Fam this is a word for the body of Christ, plain and simple. We cannot know God if we do not know His Word. I encourage everyone reading this post to get into the life saving Word of God and grow thereby. He wants to bless us even more than we could think or imagine.

I'm jus sayin...Luv me.

***

"How can a young man (old man or woman) cleanse his way? By taking heed according to Your word. With my whole heart I have sought You; Oh let me not wander from Your commandments ! Your word have I hidden in my heart that I might not sin against You."

Good morn. Fam.. You have just read Psalm 119:9-11, and I come to declare to you today that the Word works. I only ask that you take it from someone who has just about tried it all, and again my declaration to you this morning is that the Word will work for you as it has for me.

God is no respecter of person. He is not like a man, who will look at you and make a judgment about you for no good reason. God looks at the heart of man. Anyone who will choose His way will have no good thing withheld from them.

As a young man I went to church because that's what we were brought up to do. I heard bible stories and believed that they were true, but to take His Word literally was a stretch. Upon striking out on my own, I was introduced to a savior (Jesus) and accepted Him for myself. Needless to say life got better as I tasted and saw how good this Savior truly was.

Then came temptation in the form of a woman and I must be honest. I felt this new thing to me (sex), was so good that I ran after it with my whole heart. Before I knew it I had backslidden right out of the church door and far away from the Lord's house.

I truly don't have the time to tell you of all the hell I went through in the years to follow, I'll just say that it wasn't pretty, drug addictions, penitentiaries, street life, and whore mongering led me to some pretty dark places. BUT GOD, saw fit to reach out to me even in a jail cell and declare that he wasn't through with me yet. That is why you are reading these words today.

I'll leave you with this one thought. My worst day serving God was still better than my best day serving the enemy, and he wants to give each of us the abundant life 4real. So seek Him while He may be found. He can be found in the pages of His Word. After all, they are one.

I'm jus sayin...Luv me.

***

Good morning Fam..Matt.4:4 "But He answered and said, "It is written, Man shall not live by bread alone, but by every word that proceeds from the mouth of God."

Fam if you do not partake of bread and water, physical food, it is a known fact that you will starve to death.

 Many of us make claims of knowing God through salvation, yet we will never take time to feed our Spirits, by partaking of the Word. It is a sad state of affairs when we spend so much time preparing and enjoying physical food and neglect to feed our Spirit man. The above scripture came from the mouth of Jesus. It declares that it is the Word that will sustain us, not just the bread we eat. There are some of us who only crack the bible when the preacher says now let us read together. God forbid. Then we wonder why we have no victories in our lives. Why aren't we being overcomers? It is because we are starving our spirit man and not allowing Him to grow.

If we want all that God has for us, we must get to know this God we claim by studying His Word. It is imperative for your spiritual growth Fam.

I'm jus sayin...Luv me.

***

"For God so loved the world that He gave His only begotten Son, that whosoever believes in Him should not perish but have everlasting life". John 3:16

"that if you confess with your mouth the Lord Jesus and believe in your heart that God has raised Him from the dead, you will be saved. For with the heart one believes unto righteousness, and with the mouth confession is made unto salvation". Romans 10:9-10

Good morning. Fam, you've just read scriptures used in evangelism circles for years to point folks to the cross.

It has dawned on me that I have not printed the sinners prayer in some time, giving any who desires the opportunity to accept Christ. This is not something that should be taken for granted. To assume that everyone who reads these posts, or goes to a church building is saved is a deadly mistake with eternal consequences.

I've always said, going to a church building doesn't make you saved, any more than sitting in a garage makes you a car. Please read out loud so that you can hear the following prayer that I will print. Believe it in your heart and you will be saved. Your faith will make you whole.

Dear Jesus, I confess that I am a sinner. I believe in my heart that You came to earth to pay for my sins. You died as a payment for my sins and rose from the grave on the third day. I believe that right now You are seated at the right hand of the Father pleading the cases of those who trust in You. So right now I ask that You would forgive my sins and come into my heart to live forevermore. I promise to listen for Your voice and heed it in my decision making. I promise to get to know You by getting to know Your Word. With Your help from this day forward I will call You Lord. I thank You for forgiving me and trust that you are now residing in my heart. I will forever give You all the praise and honor for all that You have done and will do in my life. Thank You, in Jesus name I pray, Amen.

If you just said that prayer with your mouth and believed it in your heart you are now saved, get into the Word, specifically the Gospels, Matthew, Mark, Luke and John to find out about this Jesus that you now have a relationship with, If you need help inbox me.

I'm jus sayin...Luv me.

***

Good morning and TGIF Family.. "My brethren, count it all joy when you fall into various trials, knowing that the testing of your faith produces patience. But let patience have its perfect work, that you may be perfect and complete, lacking nothing. "James 1:2-4

Fam if we live long enough we will have trials. Some trials will seem unfair and unwarranted, but know this, This Too Shall Pass. No... trouble doesn't last always. If we would learn to count it all joy when trials come, instead of freaking out and giving up, patience is produced and you will grow in God.

Sometimes trials come at the most inopportune times. We are often caught totally off guard surmising that we don't deserve these trials, as we have been doing good in our own eyes. However, most of our trials are just a test, like the civil defense warnings on TV. They are meant to prepare you for something much bigger than you could ever anticipate, building your spiritual muscle. Therefore we must believe that if it doesn't kill you it is only meant to make you stronger.

It's Friday! As I do every week at this time, I ask, no beg you to find a body of believers, that rightly divide the Word. Join with them in offering God some corporate praise and receive the Word with gladness.

I'm jus sayin...Luv me

***

Good morning Fam. "Now faith is the substance of things hoped for the evidence of things not seen." Hebrews 11:1

"But without faith it is impossible to please Him, for he who comes to God must believe that He is, and that He is a rewarder of those that diligently seek Him." Hebrews 11:6

It is Monday and a new week and opportunity for us to get it right. I choose to walk by faith this day and not be moved by the things I see. Fam today, more than ever it is imperative that those of us who claim to know Jesus be guided by faith and not by sight. What we see will cause us to lose our focus on the promises we have received of God.

Being influenced by the things we hear will incite an atmosphere of fear. Beware of a propensity to fear. Fear is the kryptonite to our faith. It is written that "perfect love casts out fear". If we allow ourselves to walk in fear we are not operating in faith.

Whose report will you believe???

I'm jus sayin...Luv me.

***

God morning Fam. Phil. 4:6-7 "Be anxious for nothing, but in everything by prayer and supplication, with thanksgiving, let your requests be made known to God; and the peace of God, which surpasses all understanding, will guard your hearts and minds through Christ Jesus."
verse 8 "Finally, brethren, whatever things are noble, whatever things are just, whatever things are pure, whatever things are lovely, whatever things are of good report, if there is any virtue and if there is anything that is praiseworthy-meditate on these things."

Fam I sort of combined yesterday's meditations with todays. Yesterday we talked about Faith and Fear. The gist of what I spoke on is not mixing the two opposites as one cancels out the other.

Today the scriptures tell us what we must concentrate on, think on, to gain the peace of God. Life will throw us curve balls. Contrary to popular teaching, know that just because we accept Christ does not mean all of our troubles are over. The Word of God says that it will rain on the just and the unjust. That means all of us. But if we will pray in faith, and keep our minds on the things that are lovely, of good report, just, etcetera, God will keep us in perfect peace.

Isaiah 26:3 "You will keep him in perfect peace, Who's mind is stayed on You, Because he trusts in You."

Fam I leave you with this thought. It's your choice. Keep your mind on your troubles and have no peace, or keep your mind on Jesus and enjoy that peace that surpasses all understanding.

I'm jus sayin...Luv me.

***

Good morning Fam. "Then, as He was now drawing near the descent of the Mount of Olives, the whole multitude of the disciples began to rejoice and praise God with a loud voice for all the mighty works they had seen, saying: Blessed is the King who comes in the name of the Lord! Peace in heaven and glory in the highest!" and some of the Pharisees called to Him from the crowd, "Teacher rebuke Your disciples. "But He answered and said to them, "I tell you that if these should keep silent, the stones would immediately cry out". Luke 19:37-40

Fam we were born to give God praise and if we choose to keep silent about the mighty works God has done for us, the rocks will cry out for us, His creation speaks of His glorious works and the stars declare His glory. We are His most prized creation, as He made us in his image. Therefore God expects us to give Him the praise he is due. He might not have done for you the same things He has done for me, but if you will look back on your life. God has done some things for you that you could not have done for yourself, made ways out of no ways. He has brought you through some situations that there was no good end in your sight, and has said yes to you when everybody else said no. Awwww this is a good time for a praise break right here!!! Therefore you ought to give Him praises so that no rock will have to cry out for you. Make sure you praise Him for yourself. HE'S WORTHY!!!

I'm jus sayin...Luv me.

***

My Father who resides in heaven, holy and righteous is your name. Your kingdom come to this earth, and reside in me. Your will be done, in us and around us as it is in heaven. Give us this day our daily portion of Your bread of life, as well as physical sustenance for our bodies. Forgive us our trespasses as we forgive others, and give us wisdom to be forgivers 4real. Let us not be tempted Lord, above that which You can deliver us from, and when we are, make our way of escape clear, deliver us. For Yours is the Kingdom, and the glory is also Yours, for every good thing happening in our lives and we acknowledge Your Lordship as we pray in Jesus name, Amen.

"But I say to you who hear; Love your enemies, do good to those who hate you, "bless those who curse you, and pray for those who spitefully use you. To him who strikes you on the one cheek, offer the other also.(wait a minute, I don't know about that one, Jesus help me to grow) And from him who takes away your coat, do not withhold you tunic either".

Fam this morning we have read from the Beatitudes listed in Luke chapter 6. They are written in red, signifying that they are words from Jesus's mouth, Read them for yourself when you get a chance, I'm sure they will bless your life.

TGIF, and as every week at this time I ask, no beg you to find a body of believers this weekend that rightly divide the Word to join in offering God some corporate praise. Have a blessed weekend!!

I'm jus sayin...Luv me.

***

Good morning Fam. John 13:34-35 "A new commandment I give to you, that you love one another; as I have loved you, that you also love one another. By this all will know that you are My disciples, if you have love one for another."

Notice these words in red did not include judge, condemn, gossip about, point out faults or chastise. Jesus said they shall know us by our love, not by how well we expose others faults. Another scripture says that love covers a multitude of sin, when we cover something we are not exposing it, we are doing just the opposite. The church today, in this age of social media has a propensity to put peoples' problems, mistakes, miscues, and faults out there on this great information highway for the world to see.

We all have sinned and come short of the glory of God. Some of us even miss the mark a little more often than others. As Christians there are no carbon copy walks with the Lord. Yes some seem to have it all together. Every time you see them you're greeted with the standard greeting, "Hey brother/sister, I'm blessed and highly favored of the Lord". Some folks will never give you an impression that shows that they are hurting, their home life is a wreck, or maybe they've gotten themselves deep into some secret sin. No one wants to project their vulnerability and one of the main reasons is because they know that they will be exposed, instead of covered.

Shame on the church, that ain't love!

Fam let's make an effort to get our love up, THIS IS a command from God.

I'm jus sayin...Luv me.

***

"Now when the Day of Pentecost had fully come, they were all with one accord in one place. And suddenly there came a sound from heaven, as of a rushing mighty wind, and it filled the whole house where they were sitting. Then there appeared to them divided tongues, as of fire, and one sat upon each of them. And they were all filled with the Holy Spirit and began to speak with other tongues, as the Spirit gave them utterance". Acts 2:1-4

Fam today don't get it twisted, if the current day church does not have the Holy Spirit, it does not have the power to be Christ's own. It is religion based and not relation based. Tough words, but true and needed. Many in church buildings think that miracle working power is a thing of the past, reserved for people from the bible days, NOT... God wants to do even greater works through you, but we must use the tools provided, or for better wording, partake of The Helper sent to help us, THE HOLY SPIRIT.

Today is a no nonsense Word day and I know it won't be popular, but necessary it is. I'm not sorry if I stepped on your toes. Not really!

I'm jus sayin...Luv me.

***

Father God, I come to You this morning, asking that You forgive me of my sins and wash me with Your life giving blood. I thank You for every eye and heart that this prayer comes into contact with. I lift up my Fam to you today and ask that You remove from each of us anything that is unlike You. By Your Holy Spirit draw us closer to Your bleeding side that so that the blood would cover us as we go to and fro, in this world, but not of this world. Lord today I ask that Your Spirit draw all that have not accepted You. Bring them to a place in life that they would seek You and find You with all of their hearts. Cover our homes, children, and all that we claim as ours with Your mighty hand. Be with us one and all today and help us to see You in those we come in contact with. Lord when we cannot see You in them help us to share You, and allow us to be examples of Your life so that others would be drawn to YOU. It's in Jesus' name that I offer this prayer today, and I trust that You will answer in a manner that is as excellent as You are. AMEN!

***

Good morning Fam. "But those who wait on the Lord Shall renew their strength; They shall mount up on wings like eagles, They shall run and not be weary, They shall walk and not faint." Isaiah 40:31

Fam sometimes this world and all of the responsibilities required of us to survive in it, will wear us down. I must admit that sometimes I experience depression, which I know is not of God. Today's scripture says that if we wait upon the Lord, He will renew our strength.

Now it is important to know that waiting on the Lord does not mean sitting idly by, waiting on something to happen. When you go to a restaurant, notice what a waiter does. He or she doesn't sit around, they are busy serving, taking care of peoples' needs. That's what waiting on the Lord is all about, serving Him.

How do we serve or wait on God? Glad you asked. We serve God by being a servant to His people.

Matthew 25:40 "And the King will answer and say to them, Assuredly, I say to you, inasmuch as you did it to one of the least of these My brethren, you did it to me".

One might even ask who is "the least of these", and I submit to you today. The least of these are ones that everyone else looks past, street people, the homeless, the sick, drug addict, the widow, the fatherless child, the inmate. People the world overlook and cast aside as meaningless. When we do for, and serve them we are doing for God. Waiting on the Lord!

I submit to you today from experience, that there is no greater joy than the joy you receive from helping someone who has been kicked aside by the world. I have been more blessed by doing for "the least of these", than any other single thing I can think of.

I would challenge each of you to try it today, go out of your way to help someone that you wouldn't normally, someone that you might normally overlook and rush past. Go to the homeless shelter or the Micah house and give of your time and your substance, that's waiting on the Lord Fam. That will get your strength renewed!

I'm jus sayin...Luv me.

***

Good morning Fam. It is a glorious Monday, I for one am thankful to see it, therefore I will not curse the day that the Lord has made with my lips.

Fam, many of us ask God various things and wonder why we don't receive them.

 "If you abide in Me, and my Word abides in you, you will ask what you desire and it shall be done for you". John15:7

Is His word abiding in you? Contemplating the whole asking God for stuff, reading here I take it that there are requirements for us to receive from God. This requirement alone (If you abide in Me, and My Word abides in you) is enough to disqualify many of today's Christians. Sadly many times the only times we open a bible is when the preacher says turn to such and so. Sadly, many of us do not partake of the Word with regularity.

Many mornings I have written about the importance of getting to know the Word for yourself, there is absolutely no substitute for this. Hearing the preacher quote from the bible on Sunday mornings alone is not what is required of us. God is His Word!! (In the beginning was the Word, and the Word was with God, and the Word was God. John 1:1) To know God we must spend some time buried in His Word, in effect burying His Word into us.

Fam I would like to begin this week with a strong advisement, put some time in learning the Word, getting It in you. The day will come when you will need It to be able to stand and It will be the only thing to anchor you in the storms of life which will come.

I'm jus sayin...Luv me.

***

Good morning and TGIF Fam."Be anxious for nothing, but in everything by prayer and supplication, with thanksgiving, let your requests be made known to God; and the peace of God, which surpasses all understanding, will guard your hearts and minds through Christ Jesus. Finally, brethren, whatever things are true, whatever things are noble, whatever things are just, whatever things are pure, whatever things are lovely, whatever things are of good report, If there is any virtue and if there is anything that is praiseworthy- meditate on these things". Phillipians 4:6-8

What's on your mind? We are instructed in Philippians to keep our minds on things that are pure, lovely, things of good report, and if we do He will keep us free from the struggles that happen in our minds. The sin we get involved in, in most cases starts in our minds. The warfare for our souls starts in the mind. Brothers and sisters in The Lord until our minds are renewed, it is our responsibility to keep it on things of God.

As I do every week at this time, I'm asking , no begging you to find a group of believers this weekend that rightly divide the

Word to join in offering God some corporate praise.God bless you one and all!
I'm jus sayin...Luv me.

***

Good morning Fam. "And I will pray the Father, and He will give you another Helper, that He may abide with you forever, even the Spirit of truth, whom the world cannot receive, because it neither sees Him nor know Him; but you know Him, for He dwells with you and will be in you." John 14:16-17 (Found in the Bible in red letters signifying Jesus's words)
Fam I have written to you before about the third person in the godhead, The Holy Spirit. I have shared that according to the scripture that it is imperative that we be baptized in the Holy Spirit. The Holy Spirit living in us gives us the power to live in Christ and be victorious in our walk with Jesus.

Some think that this Holy Spirit AKA Holy Ghost is the goosebumps we feel when we hear a good song, sermon, or experience a movement of God in church. Others have reduced Him to a dance or a shout given when the Spirit is high.

The scripture for the day identifies the Holy Spirit spoken of as a person. Jesus said it was expedient for Him to leave the disciples. However His promise was that He would not leave us comfortless. Jesus promised to send us a Helper, Who's job it is to bring us into all truths. The Comforter would also be our guide, speaking to our hearts and spirits, guiding us along a path that we cannot see in the natural, but in the spiritual.

This Holy Spirit (helper, guide, teacher, third person of the godhead) is also the only way for us to connect with God today. The Word tells us that "no man comes to God unless the Spirit draws him". If you reach God by any other means you are a thief and a robber the Word says.

Fam today I ask you to petition God in your prayer time and ask Him to send you the Helper if you don't already have Him. It is time for us to start using the Power sent to help us. He is not a feeling, a goosebump, a good feeling, a dance, He is our Helper and we need Him, to survive.

I'm jus sayin...Luv me.

***

God morning. Fam.. "Therefore as the elect of God, holy and beloved, put on tender mercies, kindness, humility, meekness, longsuffering; bearing with one another, and forgiving one another, if anyone has a complaint against another even as Christ forgave you, so you must also do." Colossians 3:12-13

Recently I've discovered a song that was written and recorded by Kevin LaVar, about forgiveness. This song I cannot get out of my head and I believe it's because there is a need for true forgiveness in the body of Christ today.
If Jesus were to come back today, many would be left behind because of unforgiveness. The bible commands us to forgive, it's not merely a suggestion..
I know that many of you would say, but you just don't know Bro. Don what that person did to me. My question would be to you. Did they do as much to you as they did to Christ on the cross that day? Yet our example, our model for living, Jesus, forgave.

I would like to share with you some of the lyrics from the song I spoke of. I will ask you to examine yourself and check your unforgiveness. Also I beg of you to turn it over to Jesus should you find in your heart of hearts that you have an issue of unforgiveness.

"I want a heart of forgiveness, A heart full of love. One with compassion, just like Yours above. One that overcomes evil, with goodness and love, like it never happened, never holding a grudge. I want a heart that forgives, one that lives and let's live, one that keeps loving over and over again. One that man can't offend, because Your Word is deep within. One that loves without price, like You did Jesus Christ. Wanna heart that loves everybody, even my enemies.

If we can't forgive others, he cannot forgive us, it's in the Word yall.

I'm jus sayin...Luv me

***

Good morning. Fam.. I need to die!! For those of you who think that I have arrived, let me make this one announcement. I need to die to my desires that are not of God. I know that most of you have already mastered this dying to the flesh thing. However, I've got struggles (things in my flesh) that I need to die to, so that I can be all that God wants and desires for my life.

"For if you live according to the flesh you will die; but if by the Spirit you put to death the deeds of the body, you will live." "For as many as are led by the Spirit of God, these are the sons of God."
Romans 8:13

Yes Fam., we all want all that God has for us and wait with great expectation for all of the promises of God to be released into our lives. Many of us believe for big things from God and think sometimes that we've been waiting too long.

I want to share with you today that God is also waiting on some of us to let go of some things so that he can give you some of the things that He promised. Personally I've realized that there are some things I've got to let go in order to receive. If I received some of the things I've been waiting for in my present condition, they would only be squandered. Therefore my prayer is that the Lord reveals those things to me.

"By Your Holy Spirit help me to recognize and let them go. I want all that You have for me, but Lord I know also that I need to die".

How about you Fam? It's soul searching time. Self examination is a must in this walk!

I'm jus sayin...Luv me.

***

TGIF Fam. It's a holiday weekend and whether you celebrate all saints eve/Halloween or not (I choose not), please be careful as the little ones will be out. I would like to end this week with a prayer, hope it helps.

Father God I come to You this morning asking forgiveness for sins of omission as well as sins of commission. I give you all the glory as I exalt your name this morning. I declare that there is no God like You. I will exalt You at all times and declare Your works to the world. You have done for me and many, over and over again. You've exhibited Your grace in times when we didn't even care about ourselves. So I thank You. If I had a thousand tongues, it wouldn't be enough to thank and praise Your mighty works.

Right now I ask that You cover my Fam with Your arms of protection and love. Draw us each and everyone, closer to You this weekend. Cause us to thirst for You as never before. Be that force of righteousness that causes us to want to be like You.

Comfort any among us who are sick and bring peace to any who are troubled. Lord by Your Spirit move on and in us, stir us up and do not let us be comfortable with mediocrity, our own personal sins, a spirit of compromise, or anything that is contrary to Your Word and Your will.

We love You and thank You in advance for all that You will do in and through us. It's in Jesus' name we pray, Amen.

As I do every week at this time, I ask , no beg you Fam to find a body of believers that rightly divide the Word to join with. Corporately offering God praise and worship this weekend. I know just the place if you will inbox me. God bless you one and all.

Im jus sayin ...Luv me.

***

"There we also, since we are surrounded by so great a cloud of witnesses, let us lay aside every weight, and the sin which so easily ensnares us, and let us run with endurance the race that is set before us, looking unto Jesus, the author and finisher of our faith, who for the joy that was set before Him endured the cross, despising the shame, and has sat down at the right hand of the throne of God." Hebrews 12:1-2

This Word is for me Fam. If you can use it, please do.

Please pray that I be granted the strength to lay it down. Lay down what? Glad you asked. The answer is anything that would hinder the work that the Lord is trying to do in my life. The Word tells us to lay aside every weight and sin that so easily ensnares us, holds us back, hinders our walk, slows down our progress, etcetera.

The cloud of witnesses spoken of in our scripture today are the saints that have gone on before us, the disciples, and our saved loved ones. Personally, I imagine Big Mama and Aunt Rosa. They are cheering us on, saying "you can do it", "come on", "you're almost there" "don't give up now".

I am determined to be all that God wants me to be. To be that, I must lay some things and some people down. Laying aside every weight and sin that negatively affects my walk with the Lord, and ministry to His people.
I'm jus sayin...Luv me.

***

Good morning Fam. "Come unto Me all you who labor and are heavy laden, and I will give you rest. Take my yoke upon you and learn from Me, for I am gentle and lowly in heart, and you will find rest for your souls. For My yoke is easy and the burden is light." Matt.11:28

Fam this scripture speaks to all of us, especially in these times, as many are scrambling to make it. Even those who have plenty of money have to worry about how to keep it and how to spend it.

When we take the yoke of Christ upon us personally, the Lord is allowed to take His rightful place in our decision making, our choices, the way that we approach situations, including the way we handle our finances.

I have tested this scripture by trying life both ways, with God and without God. I found that without God I created my own rules to life and did what my flesh wanted. There was a certain amount of satisfaction associated with this life, but ultimately there was something missing. Eventually I ended up stressed out and beat up by a system that was not for me. Anybody that tells you that living in sin for a season is no fun is lying to you. However there is a heavy cost to pay here and now, and more importantly in eternity.

Life with God on the other hand is filled with so much less stress. I learned to cast my cares on Him. When I am walking according to His purposes, God makes my way clearer illuminating my paths. His yoke is easy and burdens made lighter.

I would not begin to tell you that all of my problems ceased the moment I trusted God. I will say that knowing Christ made them easier to handle, as He, by His Spirit speaks to my Spirit and His wisdom is infinitely superior to mine.

I'm just sayin trust God with your life by inviting Him into your heart and see for yourself.

"oh taste and see that the Lord is good; Blessed is the man who trusts in Him!". Psalm 34:8

I'm jus sayin...Luv me.

***

Good morning Fam. "By this we know love, because He laid down His life for us. And we also ought to lay down our lives for the brethren. But whoever has this world's goods, and sees his brother in need, and shuts up his heart from him, how does the love of God abide in him? My little children, let us not love in word or in tongue, but in deed and in truth." 1 John 3:16-18

Fam these are the days when our love will be put to the test. We can sit in a church building, look our neighbor in the eye and say whatever we want. That does not make our words true. It's easy to mouth the words "I love you". Saying those words for some is just hollow speaking. According to The Word of God in the scripture for today. Love is not just some warm fuzzy feeling or some verbiage to recite when commanded by a preacher.

Love is an action. Jesus proved this when He demonstrated His love by laying down His life to pay for our messes. He volunteered to suffer a horrible death when He went to the cross to pay for our sins to be a ransom for us. Yet, when some of us are asked to give up a seat, buy someone a meal, stop to be courteous, or any number of trivial things we could do to demonstrate our love, it is too much of a task and we shut up our hearts from the person in need.

We are living in the days when our love is going to be tested and tried. Sometimes the people that we will be called on to love are unloveable, but make no mistake we will be asked to go there. It is written, "let us not love in word or tongue, but in deed and in truth". 1 John 3:18

I'm Jus sayin...Luv me.

***

Yo Fam. I ain't gone nowhere. I was slow moving this AM and had to rush to leave for work.

Know this, there is no god like our God. He will not allow our feet to stray from the path (if we have chosen to follow Him). We cannot be plucked from His mighty hand. He not only has our back, but He guides our footsteps and illuminates our paths.

***

Good morning Fam. "And let us consider one another in order to stir up love and good works, not forsaking the assembling of ourselves together, as is the manner of some, but exhorting one another, and so much the more as you see the day approaching." Hebrews 10:24

Fam I hope yall went to church yesterday, I know many will say that I don't have to go to church, I can have church at home, but this verse in Hebrews chapter 10 expressly says that we are not to neglect the assembling of ourselves for the purpose of exhorting (encouraging) one another to good works and stirring up love amongst one another.

Note it did not say assemble together to see what sista so and so was wearing and who they were with, stuff to gossip about. lol

Personally I feel a burning desire to get there on Sunday mornings to gird myself up for the mess the world will surely throw at me all week long. Before going off on stupidity, when I'm in fellowship with other saints I'm more prone to pause and consider what the Lord would have me do before speaking or acting on it.

Primarily I go expecting to hear a Word from God that will help me to grow in wisdom and die to self, allowing the Spirit man to be increased in my life. Sometimes I feel like I have the propensity to be the worst of the worst so I have to feed my Spirit. Feeding it suppresses the flesh Don, that I pray most of you do not know.

I feel a strong pull to get back to encouraging in the Word this week. Stay tuned as I seek Him and report what thus sayeth the Lord to me!

I'm jus sayin...Luv me
.

***

TGIF Fam. "Therefore let him who thinks he stands take heed lest he fall. No temptation has overtaken you except such as is common to man; but God is faithful, who will not allow you to be tempted beyond what you are able, but with the temptation will also make the way of escape, that you may be able to bear it". 1 Corinthians 10:12-13

It is the weekend Fam. A time when many of us will want to let our hair down, go out and maybe be with friends and family. Some will get their party on(more than will admit 4real). That's okay, when you have a relationship with Christ as opposed to religion. God's got your back and will illuminate your paths as you go forward.

The scripture posted today I have found to be too real. I have put myself in some situations that were not conducive to my walking in right-standing in the Lord. I don't recommend that you try God or test Him at this thing, even though foolishly I have. Following the flesh I've put myself in some precarious situations and I've seen God make that way of escape even when I didn't want it.

Glory to God!!!! The situation fell apart right before my eyes and the opportunity to sin was vanquished. God is faithful to perform His Word even when we intend to disobey. He knows our hearts.

Every week at this time I ask, no beg you to find a body of believers that rightly divide the Word to join with, in offering God some corporate praise. As a matter of fact you can join me, you'll love my Pastor and the praise and worship is off the hook.

Love you one and all be blessed and be a blessing yall.

I'm jus sayin...Luv me.

***

"For by GRACE (unmerited, unearned favor) you were saved through FAITH (the substance of things hoped for, the evidence of things not seen) and not of yourselves; (you did not or can not earn it) it is the gift of God, not of WORKS, (being in the choir, willing workers club, usher board, or even the pastor's aide committee) lest anyone should boast". Ephesians 2:8

Good morning Fam. I am so glad my salvation isn't performance based. It does not hinge upon my works. I didn't earn it, could not buy it, and it doesn't depend or exist because of the great and mighty things Don has done. My salvation is a gift from God. A gift is not earned, it is only received. Some folks try to make salvation performance based. That implies if you make a mistake today you could lose your salvation, making sin stronger than salvation.

Some self-righteous folk look down their religious noses and think that surely that bum on the street won't make it into their heaven. That murderer is surely going to hell, and definitely that crackhead in your family is headed to hell in a handbasket.

That's why I rejoice in the fact that Jesus is the author and finisher of my faith and not a mere man. When I fall, or fail, I can go to Him and ask for forgiveness, expecting restoration. Man has neither a hell, nor a heaven to put me in.

Many will be surprised at who they see when they make it to heaven. Moreover, many religious folk will be astonished when they hear the words "depart from me, for I never knew you".

I'm jus sayin...Luv me

***

"Do not speak evil of one another, brethren. He who speaks evil of a brother and judges his brother, speaks evil of the law and judges the law. But if you judge the law, you are not a doer of the law but a judge. There is one Lawgiver who is able to save and to destroy. Who are you to judge another" James 4:11-12

The Word speaks for itself fam, keep your mouth off of people, and examine yourself.

I'm jus sayin….Luv me.

***

TGIF Family. "Therefore do not worry, saying, What shall we eat? or What shall we drink? or What shall we wear? For after all these things the Gentiles (non Jewish people) seek. for your heavenly Father knows that you need these things. BUT SEEK FIRST THE KINGDOM OF GOD AND HIS RIGHTEOUSNESS, AND ALL THESE THINGS SHALL BE ADDED TO YOU". Matthew 6:31-33

Fam it's the weekend and the Christmas season is underway. People are already, before Thanksgiving, starting to work themselves into a frenzy keeping up with the commercial aspect of Christmas.

This time of the year can be depressing and very stressful as folk try to keep up with the Jones, buying all the nice things they would like to see their loved ones with. Many go into a whole year's worth of debt to satisfy their desires for one day. Many others worry themselves sick because they do not know how they will pull off all of these purchases and they seek these things day and night.

Fam the word says that we should not worry about "things", but we should seek first the Kingdom of God and all His righteousness, and the things we desire (that are within His will) will be added to us. We so often get it wrong by seeking things first and attempting to get with the Kingdom business later, sort of like putting the horse before the cart.

I leave you this weekend as usual asking you to seek first the Kingdom of God. Start by joining with an assembly of folks who rightly divide the Word to offer up to God some corporate praise.

SEEK HIM FIRST FAM AND WATCH THE THINGS COME.

I'm jus sayin...Luv me.

***

Good morning Fam."For though we walk in the flesh,we do not war according to the flesh. For the weapons of our warfare are not carnal but mighty in God for pulling down strongholds, casting down arguments(refusing to argue) and every thing that exalts itself against the knowledge of God, bringing every thought into captivity to the obedience of Christ,".
2 Corinthians 10:3-5

It's Your Thinking That's Holding You Back Fam. In the rooms (N.A. & A.A.), we had a term called "Stinkin Thinkin". Stinkin Thinkin would tell you that you are clean from whatever your addiction source was. You're feeling okay now, so it's okay to go out and try "just one". Better yet now that you have gotten clean, it's okay to hang out with the same people you used to get high with, because you are now clean. Fam that's "stinkin thinkin". If you go to the barbershop enough, sooner or later you're gonna get a haircut.

None of us are exempt from trouble. Any past sin or negative condition we have been delivered from will jump on us again if we don't change our mindset, get ourselves out of positions that can lead to compromise and away from people that are still involved with the thing that we have been freed from.

The Bible calls for renewing your mind, bringing your thoughts into obedience to the knowledge of God. This has to come by the process that includes washing your mind with the water of the Word.

If you always do what you always did, you'll always get what you always got. It's been defined as insanity to expect different results doing the same things.

Finally today I ask you to consider "renewing your minds" Fam. Allow God to have control, handing over your rights to choose to Him.
I'm jus sayin...Luv me.

***

"I beseech (implore, encourage) you therefore, brethren by the mercies of God that you present your bodies a living sacrifice, acceptable to God which is your reasonable service. And do not be conformed to this world, but be transformed by the renewing of your mind, that you may prove what is that good and acceptable and perfect will of God." Romans 12:1-2

Good morning Fam. there are things in my life that seem impossible in my own power to shake. I surmise that I am akin to Paul who declared that he had a thorn in his flesh. When he petitioned God to remove it, God answered that His grace was sufficient. Now the easy way out for me is to settle for my "thorn" and "His grace". However, as I read Romans I'm told to present my body as a living sacrifice. Verse two says that I must renew my mind and not conform. How is this possible?

Fam. I submit to you today that renewing our minds is only accomplished by the washing of the Word. It is impossible to be renewed in the mind if we will not take the time to study the Word of God for ourselves. If we want to please God ultimately, we must allow Him to change us daily into His image. I wanna look like my Abba Father!

Fam., how about you?

I'm jus sayin...Luv me.

***

"Now when the day of Pentecost had fully come, they were with one accord in one place.And suddenly there came a sound from heaven, as of a rushing mighty wind, and it filled the whole house where they were sitting. Then there appeared to them divided tongues, as of fire, and one sat upon each of them. And they were all filled with the Holy Spirit and began to speak with other tongues as the Spirit gave them utterance." Acts 2:1-4

TGIF Fam."Now concerning things offered to idols; We know that we all have knowledge. Knowledge puffs up, but love edifies."
1 Corinthians 8:1

Fam I would like to leave you with a thought for the weekend. I am noticing many people scrutinizing, dissecting and in some cases folks trying to correct other folks posts. For me unless I am asked to, I will never attempt to respond to another's post with something adverse or challenging their opinion or belief. If I have another opinion and feel strongly about it I will inbox it to them, thereby not challenging them publicly.

The Word says that the world will know us by our love, not by how smart we are or how we know so much more than the next "Christian". The Word also says that we should have, or at least portray a spirit of unity, having one mind and that is the mind of Christ. As the body of Christ we need not be debating in public about differing opinions. If we have differing opinions they should be expressed in private(inboxed). This exhibits a spirit of unity to the world, even when we disagree.
We are all grown folks. Most of us, unless we solicit it, don't need to be publicly corrected. Furthermore what does that show nonbelievers?

As for me, my posts are meant to edify the body of Christ, and bring nonbelievers to the cross. If non-believers see us who claim to know Christ always debating the Word publicly, or controversially adamant about our own interpretation. Even to the point of it becoming an argument, I think it confuses folks and pushes them away from the cross. Who wants to be involved in something that the so-called established believers can't even agree on?
Don't be the one that causes a babe or a non-believer to walk away from the cross because you have an opinion that is contrary and feel a need to express it. Be kind to one another and inbox your contrary opinions and beliefs. This action at least gives the one being ministered to the appearance of the spirit of unity in the body of Christ. Be an edifier, not one so puffed up in knowledge

that you are creating confusion because you've just got to express "your" opinion.

I'm jus sayin...Luv me.

***

God Monday Fam. "Therefore gird up the loins of your mind, be sober, and rest your hope fully upon the grace that is brought to you at the revelation of Jesus Christ; as obedient children, not conforming yourselves to the former lusts, as in your ignorance; but as He who called you is holy, you also be holy in all your conduct, because it is written, be ye holy for I am holy." 1Peter 1:13-16

Fam this post is not for the faint-of-heart or any one who has not decided to go all the way with God.

WARNING: READING THIS POST MAY BE GOOD FOR YOUR HEALTH!!

Holiness, wow what an old fashioned concept. Many of us have shirked our responsibility to be holy as Grace has been extended to us over and over. We act like we can do whatever we want. Ask for forgiveness and all is good.

I am offender number one, so don't think that I am judging you. Anyone who is serious about their walk with God must first examine themselves before they can help anyone else.

Fam it is important in these last days for us to make an effort to line ourselves up with the Word. Many of us also have deleted the word repentance from our vocabulary. It has become so convenient to do our thing and depend on freely given forgiveness to cleanse us from all unrighteousness.

Repentance is having a godly sorrow for our disobedience and willfully turning from the sins we have been guilty of. We sometimes act like little children who play in the mud. God cleans us up, wipes us off and we run right back to the puddle jumping in. The modern day teachings on grace have made us so secure in God's willingness to forgive and cleanse, that we sin without conscience.

Fam in this season of Thanksgiving I will take an opportunity for self-examination. God can use what he wants, but if we make steps towards Him in repentance how much the more. Join with me, and focus on yourself and your issues. God will turn our situations around as we conform to His image.

I'm jus sayin...Luv me.

***

Good morning Fam. "And He Himself gave some to be apostles, some prophets, some evangelists, and some pastors and teachers, for the equipping of the saints for the work of the ministry, for the edifying (building up) of the body of Christ, till we all come to the unity of the faith and the knowledge of the Son of God, to a perfect man, to the measure of the stature of the fullness of Christ; that we should no longer be children, tossed to and fro and carried about with every wind of doctrine (moved by every slick word), by the trickery of men, in the cunning craftiness by which they lie in wait to deceive." Ephesians 4:11-14

Fam I apologize for the sharpness of yesterday's Word. I knew when that scripture jumped off the page at me it wasn't going to be a popular word. However obedience is better than sacrifice. I would rather give you a strong Word in obedience than to have to sacrifice.

In fact, I take that apology back. That Word on holiness was for me more than you all, and I have told you in times past that I will only give you what God gives me.

Yes my holiness has been on zero lately and I know that God is calling me to come up in Him. He has so much more for me, but He cannot release it until I am transformed in my mind and take a new attitude about sin. I am not alone, although nobody was digging what was printed yesterday, that's okay. Sometimes change isn't easy, especially with the holiday season looming in our vision.

I would guess that some of you thought that I was trying to take all of the joy out of Christmas, talkin about being Holy. I promise you that was not my intention, I was only being obedient. I reiterate it was more of a Word for me than anybody.

Be blessed Fam and don't be mad at a brother. Keep tuning in and let's see where God is taking us. Yes he loves us too much to let us stay as we are. He wants all of us to come up in Him.

I'm jus sayin...Luv me.

***

Good morning Fam, forgive me for being missing in action yesterday. Today however, is a new day. I will bless God and give Him all the praise for the mighty works He has done in my life.

"And I will pray the Father, and He will give you another Helper, that He may abide with you forever— the Spirit of truth, whom the world cannot receive, because it neither sees Him nor knows Him; but you know Him, for He dwells with you and will be in you". John 14-17

"When the Day of Pentecost had fully come, they were all with one accord in one place. And suddenly there came a sound from heaven, as of a rushing mighty wind, and it filled the whole house where they were sitting. Then there appeared to them divided tongues, as of fire, and one sat upon each of them. And they were all filled with the Holy Spirit and began to speak with other tongues, as the Spirit gave them utterance." Acts 2:1-4

When I accepted Christ into my life the very next week I came to church I found out about the Holy Spirit. What I found out was I needed Him. I found out that He is the third part of the Godhead (1.Father, 2.Son, 3.Holy Spirit). I also found that He would pray for me when I didn't know what to pray for. "Likewise the Spirit also helps in our weaknesses. For we do not know what we should pray for as we ought, but the Spirit Himself makes intercession for us with groanings which cannot be uttered". Romans 8:**26**

Finally I learned that he would be a teacher that would expose to me the mysteries of the Kingdom of God. "But the Helper, the Holy Spirit, whom the Father will send in My name, He will teach you all things, and bring to your remembrance all things that I said to you". John 14:26

You have often heard me talk of "THE POWER" that we inherit when we have been baptised in the Holy Spirit. In the greek language this power is defined as DUNAMOS power or dynamite power. This Holy Spirit that I speak about was not just for the early church, He was sent for us as well. Jesus spoke of Him as the comforter, who would bring us into all truths.

If you have not experienced the Baptism of The Holy Spirit and would like to experience Him for yourself. Ask God sincerely, He gives liberally. God knows we all need Him, especially now.

I'm jus sayin...Luv me.

***

Good morning Fam..This week we are on the subject "WORDS". The Lord is trying to show us that our words affect our lives.

"You have minds like a snake pit! How do you suppose what you say is worth anything when you are so foul-minded? It's your heart, not the dictionary, that gives meaning to your words." Matt.12:36-37

"A good person produces good deeds and words season after season. An evil person is a blight on the orchard. Let me tell you something: Every one of these careless words is going to come back to haunt you. There will be a time of Reckoning. Words are powerful; take them seriously. Words can be your salvation. Words can also be your damnation." Matt 12: 36-37(the Message bible)

Fam we have to learn to use our words to shape our lives, our destiny and our families. With the creative force of our words we have the God given authority to speak things into existence.

I know that our bank account may say that we are not rich, but the Word says that we are to "call those things that be not as though they are". Example: I speak to that bank account and command it to line up with what the Word of God says. "I am rich and I have what God says I have", "I am lacking no good thing", "I am a lender not a borrower".

Of course we have to do our parts by planting financial seeds in fruitful ministries and giving cheerfully to worthy causes, in faith.

"Do not be deceived, God is not mocked; for whatever a man sows, that he will also reap." Galatians 6:7
The Cheerful Giver] But this *I say:* He who **sows sparingly** will also reap **sparingly**, and he who **sows** bountifully will also reap bountifully. 2 Corinthians 9:6

You may be sick in your body, but you must speak health and healing to yourself. Try quoting Isaiah who says, "by His stripes we are healed".

Your kids may seem like they are demon possessed, but you must speak what you hope for their lives as opposed to what you see.

Let us practice speaking in faith today. ("Faith is the substance of things hoped for, the evidence of things not seen".) It will make a difference and if you don't see the change you desire immediately, what can you hurt?

I'm jus sayin...Luv me.

***

Good morn. and TGIF Fam..All week we have talked about the power of our words, the God given ability to create situations and atmospheres from what we say. Will we say from our mouths what God says(the truth), or will we speak on our current reality (what things look like in the natural)?

Fam I submit to you that we just ought to choose to speak the Word over our lives. If I choose to speak on my current reality life would not be painting a pretty picture. I have come a long way from where I've been, but I am nowhere near where I know by faith God is taking me, and neither are you.

"For our light affliction, which is but for a moment, is working for us a far more exceeding and eternal weight of glory, while we do not look at the things which are seen, but at the things which are not seen. For the things which are seen are temporary, but the things which are not seen are eternal." 2 Cor.4:17-18

I will leave you this week with a few quotes that you might practice saying over your life to create the life God destined for you.

*"I am the head not the tail, the first not the last".
*"I am created in the image of God and I am not a mistake".
*"I am a lender, not a borrower".
*"I am healed and whole in Jesus name".
*"My God shall supply ALL my needs according to His riches in glory".
*"I will have heaven here on earth and not just in the great by and by".
*"If God is for me who can be against me".
*"Greater is He who is in me than he who is in the world".
*"I am a joint heir with Christ and have access to the very throne of God".
*"God isn't mad with me, but madly in love with me".

Fam make a practice of speaking life over and into your life, it may sound foolish, but it works.

I'm jus sayin......Luv me.

***

Good morning Fam.."Who would dare even to point a finger? The One who died for us—who was raised to life for us!—is in the presence of God at this very moment sticking up for us. Do you think anyone is going to be able to drive a wedge between us and

Christ's love for us? There is no way! Not trouble, not hard times, not hatred, not hunger, not homelessness, not bullying threats, not backstabbing, not even the worst sins listed in Scripture: They kill us in cold blood because they hate you. We're sitting ducks; they pick us off one by one. None of this fazes us because Jesus loves us. I'm absolutely convinced that nothing—nothing living or dead, angelic or demonic, today or tomorrow, high or low, thinkable or unthinkable—absolutely nothing can get between us and God's love because of the way that Jesus our Master has embraced us." Romans 8:32 The Message Bible

The Message Bible speaks this morning Fam and it's message is clear. God knew all of your faults before He chose you, yet He chose YOU. Get your mind made up to let nothing separate you from His love. He is not mad at you, He is madly in love with YOU.

I'm jus sayin....Luv me.

***

Good morning Fam.. Only God's grace and mercy saw this day, I couldn't, I wanted to die. I wanted to end it all, BUT GOD!!!!

You too may have lost hope. Your days may seem dark and lonely. You also might have been persuaded by the enemy to end it all, BUT GOD!! Read what I read this morning, it's from the Message Bible, and I pray that it causes hope to rise up in you.

"I love God because he listened to me, listened as I begged for mercy. He listened so intently as I laid out my case before him. Death stared me in the face, hell was hard on my heels. Up against it, I didn't know which way to turn; then I called out to God for help: "Please, God!" I cried out. "Save my life!" God is gracious—it is he who makes things right, our most compassionate God. God takes the side of the helpless; when I was at the end of my rope, he saved me." Psalm 116:1-2 The Message Bible

I'm jus sayin...Luv me.

***

Good morning Fam.."And let us not grow weary while doing good, for in due season we shall reap if we do not lose heart." Galatians 6:9

Fam even while doing your best to do what's right, sometimes you will feel like quitting. Discouragement will come your way and you will feel like "what's the use". Sometimes it seems like unbelievers are prospering more, having more fun and your efforts to "do the right thing" are just not worth the struggle.

Paul wrote in his letter to the Galatians of this very thing. He admonished them to not grow weary while doing good. Just like in today's times. I imagine believers trying to do what's right watching as unbelievers seem to be having all the fun, doing good and prospering. While doing everything but what is right.

Well the good news is if we don't faint, quit, give up, walk away from the struggle or throw in the towel, HARVEST TIME IS COMING. "For God is a rewarder of those that diligently seek Him". "In due season we shall reap a righteous harvest". Then the unbeliever will know that our harvest was a result of God's goodness and be drawn to Him.

Fam., I would like to encourage someone today. Keep on fighting and keep on doing what thus says the Lord. In spite of your discouragement now, you will reap a harvest that will make you know it was worth every tear, every disappointment, every heartache.

I'm jus sayin...Luv me.

***

"And then I will declare to them, 'I never knew you; depart from Me, you who practice lawlessness!" Matthew 7:23

Good morning Fam.. I declare to you this morning that the time is upon us to be sure of our salvation. The signs of Jesus's coming are in our face and although we can say that these signs have been shown for centuries, I believe that His second coming is near.

If you will go back on my posts to the beginning of the year, you will read that I was given dreams of us living in the times spoken of as the great tribulation. During these times there will be no church as we now know it. Carrying a bible and openly speaking of Jesus will not be permitted. This is why I beg of you to hide the Word in your hearts this no one can take from you.
"Your word I have hidden in my heart, That I might not sin against You." Psalm 119:11

Another verse in the bible tells us "to work out our own souls' salvation with fear and trembling". Notice it's your soul's salvation. Your spirit is saved when you accept Christ. Your soul is saved daily, as You work it out and sometimes that happens while you are in fear and trembling. This walk requires of us to keep moving forward, even when we are afraid.

Practicing "church" and all the nuances of being churched will cause many of us to hear the aforementioned speech, "depart from me". I pray that will not be your, or better yet our experience. I want to know Him, have a relationship with Him and be welcomed into heaven by Him when my time comes.

I'm jus sayin.....Luv me.

***

Good morning. Fam.. This will be a word only morning. I can talk until I'm blue in the face, but it's the word of God that matters most. Let us today look into the mirror of the Word and I beg of you to clean up any mess you see when you look into this mirror and not just walk away from it unchanged.

"Offer to God thanksgiving, And pay your vows to the Most High. Call upon Me in the day of trouble; I will deliver you, and you shall glorify Me."

But to the wicked God says: "What right have you to declare My statutes, Or take My covenant in your mouth, Seeing you hate instruction And cast My words behind you? When you saw a thief, you consented with him, And have been a partaker with adulterers. You give your mouth to evil, And your tongue frames deceit. You sit and speak against your brother; You slander your own mother's son. These things you have done, and I kept silent; You thought that I was altogether like you; But I will rebuke you, And
set them in order before your eyes.

"Now consider this, you who forget God, Lest I tear you in pieces, And there be none to deliver: Whoever offers praise glorifies Me; And to him who orders his conduct aright I will show the salvation of God." Psalm 50:14-23

***

Good morning Fam.. "And as it is appointed for men to die once, but after this the judgment," Heb.9:27.

Fam we all have an appointment with death. It is inescapable, inevitable and we never know when it is going to happen. That's why it is important to know that you know, you have accepted Christ into your hearts so that you will also know where you will spend eternity.

I have attended funerals where the preacher gives scriptures like "to be absent from the body is to be present with the Lord". These words give the family hope that the person in "the box" is now in heaven. These are also comforting words that help the survivors to cope with their loss, allowing them to have hope in the troubled times they face. However, know this, if the person has not asked Jesus into their hearts, he or she might stand before Jesus and hear the words "depart from me".

Our eternities should not be left up to chance. It is true that on our dying beds, no matter how vile a life we have lived, we can call upon Jesus and have our slates cleaned as if we've never sinned. Many have passed up chances to accept Christ, thinking that they will live to a ripe old age, only to die unexpectedly. Don't let that be your fate Fam.. Call upon the Lord while He may be found, because you never know when or how you will be called to eternity.
I'm jus sayin...Luv me.

***

Good morning Fam.. "For He says:" In an acceptable time I have heard you, And in the day of salvation I have helped you." Behold, now is the accepted time; behold, now is the day of salvation." 2Corinthians 6:2

Fam. this message today is for all who claim to know Christ as Lord and Saviour. "NOW IS THE DAY OF SALVATION."It is time for the body of Christ to take advantage of any opportunity to minister salvation to the lost.

The world is full of people dying without having been given the opportunity to accept Christ. The sad part or reality of this is that many of us who claim to know Jesus and have experienced salvation are not sharing Christ when given the opportunity. Even sadder is the fact that when we have that chance and do not take advantage of it, if that person (that we had a chance to minister to) dies, his or her blood will be required at your hands.

Yes, this is some strong talk today and I won't apologize for posting it. We as Christians need to wake up and learn how to share salvation with the lost. We can no longer go on the assumption that we have plenty of time to talk to Sally or John. It is what we call in sports, "crunch time".

I will be sharing "The Roman Road to Salvation" with you this week". It is imperative that we take notes and at least attempt to share this and any other method to lead folks to Christ. How can they know if they are not taught?

I'm jus sayin.....Luv me.

***

Good morning Fam.. " Brethren, my heart's desire and prayer to God for Israel (everyone)is that they may be saved." Rom. 10:1

Fam as I stated yesterday we will be going over the Roman Road to salvation, just one of the bible ways to lead folks to Christ. I started by putting the first verse on the first page of my bible and the next verse on each found page. Let's get busy, being about our Father's business.

*1John 1:8 "If we say that we have no sin, we deceive ourselves, and the truth is not in us".

*Romans 3:23 "for all have sinned and fall short of the glory of God"
*1John 1:9 "If we confess our sins, He is faithful and just to forgive us our sins and to cleanse us from all unrighteousness".
*Roman 6:23 "For the wages of sin is death, but the gift of God is eternal life in Christ Jesus our Lord".
*John 3:36 "He who believes in the Son has everlasting life; and he who does not believe the Son shall not see life, but the wrath of God abides on him".
*John 3:18 "He who believes in Him is not condemned; but he who does not believe is condemned already, because he has not believed in the name of the only begotten Son of God".
*John 3:16 "For God so loved the world that He gave His only begotten Son, that whoever believes in Him should not perish but have everlasting life".
*Romans 10:13 "For whoever calls on the name of the LORD shall be saved".
*Romans 10:9-10 "that if you confess with your mouth the Lord Jesus and believe in your heart that God has raised Him from the dead, you will be saved. For with the heart one believes unto righteousness, and with the mouth confession is made unto salvation".

We will finish this road tomorrow. Please record these scriptures and use them to lead folks to the Saviour you know. Fam it's time to be about the Father's business.

I'm jus sayin....Luv me.

***

Good morn. Fam.. Yesterday we started on the Roman Road to salvation, a tool to use for leading folks to Christ. I do pray that you copied and put every scripture in your bible for easy access. Today we will finish the scripture portion from where we left off.

The last scripture was Romans 10:9-10. Today we will start with the next scripture in the Roman Road and finish up.

*Isaiah 55:6 "Seek the LORD while He may be found, Call upon Him while He is near".
*James 4:14 "whereas you do not know what will happen tomorrow. For what is your life? It is even a vapor that appears for a little time and then vanishes away".
*Revelation 3:20 "Behold, I stand at the door and knock. If anyone hears My voice and opens the door, I will come in to him and dine with him, and he with Me".
*Revelation 3:22 "He who has an ear, let him hear what the Spirit says to the churches."

Fam this is the last installation of scripture references in The Roman Road. The only thing left is to share with the person in reciting the "Sinners Prayer". I will print a version of it tomorrow, but know this, there is no one absolute correct way to share it yet there is a formula that lots of people follow.

Come back tomorrow and let's get ready for battle, leading folks into the kingdom, being about our father's business.

I'm jus sayin.....Luv me.

***

Good morning and TGIF Fam.. We started out this week making a claim that my posts were aimed at Christians sharing The Roman Road to salvation. This is a scriptural formula to share our faith with nonbelievers. Please go back to those posts and write those scriptures in your bibles and lead someone to Christ, for Christ's sake. Today I will share with you a sinner's prayer for salvation. The total object is to get the person you are witnessing to, to speak aloud this prayer. With the heart man believes, but with the mouth confession is made into salvation.

Anyone reading the following prayer out loud, while believing it in their hearts will be saved. I invite ALL to read it aloud.

Dear Jesus, I admit that I am a sinner. I ask that You would forgive me of my sins and come into my heart right now. I confess that You are the Son of God, that you died and rose again to pay for my sins. Right now, I renounce the works of the enemy and turn my life over to You. I ask You to speak to my heart and guide me in Your ways from this day forth. I vow to listen to Your Holy Spirit and pray for the wisdom to do what He says. I thank You for coming into my life and making me a new creature. In Jesus' name I pray, AMEN.

Anyone praying this prayer and believing it in their hearts will be saved. They might not feel saved, but it is no longer about their feelings it is about FAITH. Suggest they get their Faith up by hearing the Word of God. "So then Faith comes by hearing, and hearing by the Word of God". Romans 10:17

Christians let's get to work!

I'm jus sayin...Luv me.

***

Good morning Fam.." But be doers of the word, and not hearers only, deceiving yourselves. For if anyone is a hearer of the word and not a doer, he is like a man observing his natural face in a mirror; for he observes himself, goes away, and immediately forgets what kind of man he was. But he who looks into the perfect law of liberty and continues in it, and is not a forgetful

hearer but a doer of the work, this one will be blessed in what he does."
James 1:22-25

It's Monday and many of us went to church yesterday, got our praise on, and heard a good word that made us feel real good. Many of us, then left church determined to walk out what we heard.

Often after these great anointed services we leave the church and LIFE happens. Most of us have to go back to places where our unsaved, unchurched families and friends reside. The atmosphere around them is far from what we just experienced in church. If we are not watchful we forget all that we experienced in church and resort back to the comfortable, what we are used to.

James speaks of this behaviour as deceiving ourselves. He says that it is akin to looking in the mirror, seeing a mess in your eye or dirt on your face and walking away without washing away the mess. Who would do that?

The true blessing comes when we start to measure our lives by the Word, taking a personal honest inventory and allowing God to change us. It's a process that doesn't happen overnight, but believe me GOD IS ABLE.

Let's be doers of the Word, not just hearers Fam..

I'm jus sayin...Luv me.

***

Good morning Fam.."Have the same mind in you that was in Christ Jesus". Phillipians 2:5

Fam this is what we were/are called to do! There are no ifs, ands or buts about it. We are called to have the same mind in us that was in Christ Jesus.

I know that somebody did you wrong, used you, took your kindness for weakness, stole from you and talked about you behind your back. SO WHAT!!! Who do you belong to? How would Jesus handle the situation?

[Suffering for Doing Good]Summing up: Be agreeable, be sympathetic, be loving, be compassionate, be humble. That goes for all of you, no exceptions. No retaliation. No sharp-tongued sarcasm. Instead, bless—that's your job, to bless. You'll be a blessing and also get a blessing. Whoever wants to embrace life and see the day fill up with good, Here's what you do: Say nothing evil or hurtful; Snub evil and cultivate good; run after peace for all you're worth. God looks on all this with approval, listening and responding well to what he's asked; But he turns his back on those who do evil things." 1 Peter 3:8 The Message Bible

I'm jus sayin…Luv me.

***

Good morning Fam.. "I am the LORD, that is My name; And My glory I will not give to another, Nor My praise to carved images." Isaiah 42:8

Fam. I submit to you today, your giving praise to God is not an option. You cannot please Him if you are not a praiser. This very act is the only thing God needs from us. If we don't give our praise to Him, we'll give it to something or someone else and the rocks will cry out for us.
Our God is omnipotent (all powerful), omniscient(all knowing) and omnipresent(always present). He has all the power, knows

everything and is everywhere. The bible says that "the earth is the Lord's and the fullness thereof", and that means that He owns everything.

However, God is a complete gentleman that gives us the free will to accept or reject Him. He also allows us to choose whether we will give Him what He needs "our praise". Or will we praise as Isaiah says, the carved or created images.

Today our carved images or idols include things like our tech toys, our cars, homes, possessions, people, jobs, money (a major one) and clothing. The things that the world put so much importance on we will find ourselves speaking on. How many times have you told friends and family about your bad ride, exquisite home, your fly shoes, great job or even your ties to someone deemed important? That, I submit, is giving praise to carved images, things that we idolize.

God says He ain't having it. Furthermore, God inhabits (lives in) the praises of His people, His very presence resides in our praise. When we refuse to praise Him we are shutting out His presence. Are we shutting out the presence of God by praising things, people, possessions? God forbid!

I'm jus sayin...Luv me.

***

Good morning Fad. Wow the weekend went so fast, I think we need another day added, lol.

"To everything there is a season, A time for every purpose under heaven:" Ecclesiastes 3:1

Fam. we're gonna keep it simple this week and start the week with a simple truth. There is a proper time for everything, even work, lol. As a matter of fact, I am an advocate for a national retirement by age twenty. (lol) However the Bible says that if a man doesn't work he doesn't eat. Therefore my attitude about Monday morning returning to the job had to change. With the unemployment rate being so high in these economic times, I have come to the place where I am grateful for a job to go to.

It is true that I feel underpaid and that folks just don't see what I bring to the table. In the natural (the carnal man) I feel justified by murmuring and complaining, but then I consider the Word of God. In it I see what happened to the children of Israel who murmured and complained. They got stuck walking in the same circles (in the wilderness) for forty years and many never saw the promised land.

Nope, I think that isn't for me. Instead of that fate I will praise God, even when I feel like the world has dumped on me. I know that my praise pleases God and will move His hand in my favor. When He opens a door for me, no man can shut it. I said I would keep it simple this week, let's see how it goes.
I'm jus sayin...Luv me.

***

Good morning Fam.. I am truly overwhelmed to awaken to so many birthday wishes. Thank you all so much and to those who have yet to do so, I say thank you in advance.

On this day I would like to share a simple word, TRANSFORMATION. In my comment will be the Message Bible take on Romans 12:1-2. I think that we all ought to be cognizant of God's shaking that brings TRANSFORMATION. Embrace it and do not fear "the process" that we all must go through and many of us are still going through.

"So here's what I want you to do, God helping you: Take your everyday, ordinary life—your sleeping, eating, going-to-work, and walking-around life—and place it before God as an offering. Embracing what God does for you is the best thing you can do for him. Don't become so well-adjusted to your culture that you fit into it without even thinking. Instead, fix your attention on God. You'll be changed from the inside out. Readily recognize what he wants from you, and quickly respond to it. Unlike the culture around you, always dragging you down to its level of immaturity, God brings the best out of you, develops well-formed maturity in you." Romans 12:1-2 (The Message)

I'm jus sayin...Luv me.

***

Good morning Fam.. Many times I have been led to give you the sincere "milk" of the Word, but today we will dine on "meat". This will not be a popular word, but if you embrace it, it will bring life and that more abundantly.

"There is therefore now no condemnation to those who are in Christ Jesus, who do not walk according to the flesh, but according to the Spirit. For the law of the Spirit of life in Christ Jesus has made me free from the law of sin and death. For what the law could not do in that it was weak through the flesh, God did by sending His own Son in the likeness of sinful flesh, on account of sin: He condemned sin in the flesh, that the righteous requirement of the law might be fulfilled in us who do not walk according to the flesh but according to the Spirit. For those who live according to the flesh set their minds on the things of the flesh, but those who live according to the Spirit, the things of the

Spirit. For to be carnally minded is death, but to be spiritually minded is life and peace. Because the carnal mind is enmity against God; for it is not subject to the law of God, nor indeed can be. So then, those who are in the flesh cannot please God". Romans 8:1-8

Many Christians quote the first part of the above scripture, "There is therefore now no condemnation to those who are in Christ Jesus". This is to make themselves feel better about their lack of maturity in Christ and habitually giving in to their fleshly desires fueling their propensity to sin.

The second part of this mighty scripture says that this promise is for those who do not walk after the flesh (carnally minded Christians). If we walk after the things of the flesh, according to the Word, we can expect condemnation (condemnation comes from the enemy, conviction comes from the Holy Spirit).

Fam. we can't pick and choose the parts of scripture that suits our choices. The whole Word of God or none at all!

I'm jus sayin...Luv me.

***

Good morning Fam.. As promised we are going over the difference between the "carnal Christian" and the Christian who walks "after the Spirit."

"So then, those who are in the flesh cannot please God." Romans 8:8
"For those who live according to the flesh set their minds on the things of the flesh, but those who live according to the Spirit, the things of the Spirit."Romans 8:5

These verses make a clear distinction between the carnal man (one who minds the things of the flesh) and the man who minds the things of the Spirit. The carnal Christian is more interested in doing and feeding things that appeal to his or her flesh.

What do I mean? Glad you asked.
Our flesh will cause us to feed our own personal lusts (sex, greed, quest for possessions, drugs, MONEY, alcohol, etcetera) more, more, more is our cry. The more we get the more we want, we can never be satisfied. Once we get what we think we want the newness of that wears off, then we've got to have more. I liken that behavior with my days of being a Heroin addict. I was constantly chasing that ever elusive "first high". Hell or high water I was going to get it and I only went down, down, down, much like a dog chasing his own tail.

Romans 8:12-14 sums it up like this."Therefore, brethren, we are debtors—not to the flesh, to live according to the flesh. For if you live according to the flesh you will die; but if by the Spirit you put to death the deeds of the body, you will live. For as many as are led by the Spirit of God, these are sons of God."

Let that marinate in your Spirit.

I'm jus sayin...Luv me.

***

Good Monday Fam.. " The Spirit of the LORD is upon Me, Because He has anointed Me To preach the gospel to the poor; He has sent Me to heal the brokenhearted, To proclaim liberty to the captives And recovery of sight to the blind, To set at liberty those who are oppressed; To proclaim the acceptable year of the LORD." Luke 4:18-19

These words are written in red in my bible, indicating they are spoken from the mouth of Jesus. This commission was also given to all who have accepted Jesus as Lord and Savior. He commanded His followers to "go into all the world spreading the good news of the gospel".

Your world may be your job, the grocery store, the doctors office, etcetera. Spreading the gospel doesn't always mean beating folks down with the scriptures. The gospel has been defined as "the good news of what Jesus has done for you".

There is a time for you to speak the Word, but some folks will only receive the gospel that they see in your way of life. The example you show in how you deal with folks and handle situations is all the gospel some will receive. It kills me to see folks quoting the Word and the next moment talking down about someone, killing folks with words, could you see Jesus doing that? I don't think so. It reminds me of that terrible philosophy many of us heard as kids, "Do as I say, not as I do".

Fam sometimes the examples we portray will win or lose someone for the Kingdom. Make it GOOD!!

I'm jus sayin...Luv me.

***

Good morning Fam.. Let's get right to the point today.

"But why do you judge your brother? Or why do you show contempt for your brother? For we shall all stand before the judgment seat of Christ. For it is written:"As I live, says the LORD, Every knee shall bow to Me, And every tongue shall confess to God. So then each of us shall give account of himself to God. Therefore let us not judge one another anymore, but rather

resolve this, not to put a stumbling block or a cause to fall
in our brother's way." Rom.14:10-13

Fam this is a sore spot for me. Excuse me if it sounds a little
personal. I can't stand self-righteous, finger pointing, know-it-all,
so called Christians. Some folks think that it is their job to point
out everybody else's faults, expose every ministry that they think
is not correct and as the bible says, "remove the speck out of their
brother's eye", while the board is in their own eye.

I've got enough issues of my own to deal with and I'm sure that all
of us, no matter how far we've come, "have bones in our own
closets". Therefore I've surmised that I've got to spend my time on
self-examination, not examining others. When Jesus actually
returns, I promise you that in His presence we will be on our
knees, face to the carpet, tears streaming, nose running and crying
out.

We'd better learn how to get in His presence now, instead of
getting in everybody's business.

I'm jus sayin...Luv me.

***

Good morning Fam.. This has truly been a trying week; it seems
like troubles are mounting up and trying to overtake a brother. If I
were to try to handle this week in my own strength I would be
throwing in the towel, quitting and questioning God. However, the
Holy Spirit is prompting me to "count it all joy".

"My brethren, count it all joy when you fall into various
trials, knowing that the testing of your faith produces
patience. But let patience have its perfect work, that you may be
perfect and complete, lacking nothing." James 1:2-4

Fam we all have a choice. Today I choose to trust God over my circumstances, over my job, my future, my shortcomings and especially over my family. When all hell is breaking out around me I will not resort back to my old way of doing things. I will handle situations by seeking out what the Word says about them.

I was cursed and lied on just last night by someone who most would think should be close to me. Did it hurt? Yes, but the Word tells me to bless those that curse you. I want to curse them back, oh that would make my flesh feel really good, but my reward is in doing things God's way. So instead I will bless them and pray for them. It's my job to forgive.

Fam we have a choice. Our way or God's way.
I'm jus sayin...Luv me.

***

Good morning Fam.. It's been a good week, "not easy", but good. God has shown Himself strong in my life and I pray the same has been true for you. When I say "not easy", I mean there have been challenges. In those challenges by choosing God's way of handling them, He has made my yoke easy and my burdens light.

CHOICES YALL
I guess the most important thing I've had to do this week was forgive. Forgive folks that were very close to me and hurt me beyond understanding. Know this Fam, it ain't what they did that mattered, it's what I did, how I responded to their actions. Whose way did I choose to obey? I chose to obey what God's Word said to do. The carnal me wanted to go slam off and get even, but the Spiritual man said "FORGIVE".

The lesson learned Fam. No one, nor misdeed done to you is worthy of blocking your blessings, by holding onto unforgiveness.

If you can't forgive, God can't forgive you. Never give anybody that kind of power over you.

"CHOICES"

Well, the weekend is here. I would like to ask, no beg of each of you to find a body of believers that rightly divide the Word of God to join in offering God some corporate praise. Get in His face because He inhabits the praises of His people.

I'm jus sayin...Luv me.

***

Good Monday Morn. Fam.. Today I am so grateful to God for giving me the strength and wisdom to run to My safe place yesterday to receive a Word. That Word explained to me why I was going through so much "hell" last week. I thank God for my Pastor, who spoke directly to me in his sermon.

If you'll go to my page and go back, you'll see that last week was a week that I didn't totally understand all the whys to. Now I KNOW exactly what was going on and as usual, I'll share it just in case you can use it.
One thing that is true is that the enemy uses the same old tactics he has used for years against the body of Christ, today.

For all of us there is seed time (the place where you plant your seed, looking for an expected harvest). Then there's harvest time (where you expect to reap the rewards of your planting of seed). In the place in time between seedtime and harvest time is where the enemy loves to take up residence, to discourage you and keep you from receiving your harvest.
This place is truly reserved for Judah (your PRAISE) and it's the enemies desire to steal or block your praise, by distracting you

with problems, issues, temptations, etcetera. When it seems that in spite of your efforts to do the right thing, serve God and His people, and all Hell is breaking out around you. Do not allow the enemy to steal or distract your PRAISE.

Fam your harvest is coming, but between seed time and harvest time is the place that belongs to Judah, your praise!! Let it flow and clear your way to your harvest!

I don't think God is finished with this subject, let's see what tomorrow brings.

I'm jus sayin...Luv me.

***

Good morning Fam.. This week we have been talking about seed time, harvest time and more importantly how the enemy tries to block us from receiving our harvest by stopping our praise. Sadly many of us don't understand what seed sowing is all about. It's not my desire to speak about things that are foreign with you therefore let us explore sowing seed.

"Do not be deceived, God is not mocked; for whatever a man sows, that he will also reap". Galatians 6:7

Whatever you choose to sow, you will also reap. Some choose to sow seeds of love, kindness, forgiveness, patience, money, service and on and on. According to the Word they will reap a harvest according to what they have sown. Others choose to sow seeds of discord (division), gossip, backbiting, slandering, lying, cheating, (I think you should get the idea), but whatever it is that you sow you should expect to get a harvest of.
I'm jus sayin...Luv me.

***

Good morning and TGIF Fam.. This has been an awesome week of instruction from the Lord. I pray that each of you would go back on my page to pick up what you might have missed.

The gist of what we have shared this week came from a sermon my Pastor preached on Sunday. I thank God for using him. I also thank him for being open to us sharing, encouraging us to take it to the world.

When we receive knowledge (teaching) from the Lord it is imperative for us to pass it on Fam.. Otherwise we become spiritually obese, stagnated and die spiritually. This has been the ruin of many Christians as they tried to hold onto knowledge, without sharing what "thus says the Lord".

In summary we have, this week, shared on how the enemy loves to take up camp in the place between your seed sowing and your harvest. This place belongs to Judah (your praise) and let no opposition, circumstance, person or thing stop your praise. It (your praise) is a weapon and the only thing God needs from you. Be blessed and find a group of people that rightfully divide the Word to join in offering God some corporate praise this weekend. He inhabits the praises of His people.

I'm Jus sayin...Luv me.

***

Good morning Fam.. "Praise the Lord". This morning I declare that I love the Lord and His praise shall continually be in my mouth. I will praise Him in the morning, praise Him in the noonday, when I feel good and when I feel bad. I know that my praise is my weapon and my warfare is not with flesh and blood.

"For though we walk in the flesh, we do not war according to the flesh. For the weapons of our warfare are not carnal (fleshly) but mighty in God for pulling down strongholds, casting down arguments and every high thing that exalts itself against the knowledge of God, bringing every thought into captivity to the obedience of Christ," 2 Cor.10:3-5

Having an understanding of this scripture assures me that when the enemy uses people to attack me, slander me, curse me or use me. I am not to look at that person as if he or she is in control of their own actions. I should pray for that person for they have only been the instrument that the enemy used to try to get to me and try my faith.

When we make proclamations that we will serve the Lord and obey His Word, look out. The enemy is going to try that proclamation and he'll use those closest to you to do it. So instead of cursing, try praising Fam. Your praise is the most powerful weapon you have.

I'm jus sayin...Luv me.

***

Good morning Fam.. "I am the true vine, and My Father is the vinedresser. Every branch in Me that does not bear fruit He takes away; and every branch that bears fruit He prunes, that it may bear more fruit." John 15:1-2

Fam., can you stand the pruning of the Lord? Pruning hurts! However, if you are "in the Lord" and bearing fruit you will be pruned, so that you can bear more fruit."
The Lord used an unnamed TV evangelist to provide the gist of this message. I want to thank both the Lord and him.

Fam, if you are in the Lord stay faithful when He takes His pruning shears to your life. As sure as he is God and you are alive you will go through a pruning process. Pruning requires a cutting, taking away, surgery if you will and anyone who has been through a surgery will tell you that it hurts.

Part of the procedure involved in having surgery has to do with cutting. When God puts us through pruning, we may lose a child(God forbid), a job, a family member, material possessions, etcetera, but He is doing that (the pruning) so that He can give you "MORE".

God needs to know that you can handle the pain of temporary loss and still remain friends with Him, so that He can increase your territory.

I've gotta tell you the truth. When God took my first wife, I pretty much told God that we were no longer friends. Therefore, cutting my ties to God. But God in His infinite wisdom wouldn't let me go, "GLORY".

He protected me as I went through the valley of the shadow of death wanting to take my own life. In the midst of my pain and even denying him access I must admit, God wouldn't let me go. God must be true to His Word. If you abide in Him, pruning time is coming. Stay faithful, more is coming!

I'm jus sayin...Luv me.

***

Good morning Fam.. I am painfully aware of the deaths of two people I know and love this week. You may have lost a loved one as well and feel saddened by your loss. In the midst of our hurts we must still abide in the Lord and trust His plan. Yesterday we talked about the Lord's pruning. We mentioned how He must take away things to bring us increase and bear more fruit.

Let us go to the Word. "I am the true vine, and My Father is the vinedresser. Every branch in Me that does not bear fruit He takes away; and every branch that bears fruit He prunes, that it may bear more fruit." John 15:1-2

Granted, pruning or God's taking away doesn't make us feel good while we are in "the process". Let us now see what happens when we, in spite of our pain, remain in or ABIDE IN HIM.

"Abide in Me, and I in you. As the branch cannot bear fruit of itself, unless it abides in the vine, neither can you, unless you abide in Me. "I am the vine, you are the branches. He who abides in Me, and I in him, bears much fruit; for without Me you can do nothing. If anyone does not abide in Me, he is cast out as a branch and is withered; and they gather them and throw them into the fire, and they are burned. If you abide in Me, and My words abide in you, you will ask what you desire, and it shall be done for you." John 15:4-7

Glory to God, my hope is in this written Word. If I fail, I will fail holding onto the promises written in it. This Word says that even though He takes away (pruning) from me, if I ABIDE in Him, I will arrive at a place where I can ask what I desire, and it will be done. GLORAAAY!!

I am sorry but not sorry for my excitement. I can't help but believe and take God at His Word. I get excited when I dig in and discover the little nuggets of gold hidden in the Word and this is one.

"HALLELUJAH" My pain now is gonna pay later, if I Abide in Him. Don't quit, Abide. Don't become weary while doing good, Abide. When you're hurt by the people you think should be on your team, Abide.

I'm jus sayin...Luv me.

***

Good morning and TGIF Fam.. Yesterday I went to one of the best funerals I have ever been to. The only thing not good was the fact that I was there to bury a friend, Jermaine Samuels, who I feel left us way too soon. For me this ceremony gave me closure. I found out that Jermaine had accepted Christ in his life. I now have no doubt about where Young World now resides. A single decision that he made bought him a ticket to eternal life with Christ.

Another reason for my joy concerning this funeral service was that many others made the decision to allow Christ into their hearts. I applaud the preacher who gave the invitation and even more so all who were brave enough to go forward and invite Jesus into their hearts.

Today I will extend that invitation. If you will confess this prayer with your mouth and believe it in your hearts, You too can have eternal life with Jesus.

Lord Jesus, I know that I am a sinner and I believe that you are the son of God sent to pay for my sins. I ask You now to forgive me of my sins. Wash me with Your precious blood and accept me into Your kingdom. By Your Holy Spirit teach me and by Your Word guide me into Your ways of doing things. I vow to do my best to follow You from this day forward. I thank You for hearing and forgiving me this day. In Jesus name I pray. AMEN!!

Glory to God!! If you said that prayer, you are saved! Find a bible and get to know the savior that you invited into your heart. Inbox me if you need help, I'm here for you.
I'm jus sayin...Luv me.

***

Good morning Fam.. "He said to him the third time, "Simon, son of Jonah, do you love Me?" Peter was grieved because He said to him the third time, "Do you love Me?" And he said to Him, "Lord, You know all things; You know that I love You." Jesus said to him, "Feed My sheep." John 21:17

Jesus was saying to Peter that if he loved Him, he, Peter must feed His (Jesus's) sheep. Today I will ask you Fam.. Do you love Jesus? If you love Jesus it is your job to feed His sheep, teach those young in Christ. Many ministries have been guilty of leading folks to Christ and leaving them to fend for themselves.

Unfortunately many have come to Christ pronouncing the "sinners prayer" with a sincere heart of repentance, just to return to the places where they come from with no spiritual guidance. In the absence of an example, the same negative influences eventually conform one to the lifestyles they are used to.

To win a soul for Christ is an amazing thing, but we also have a responsibility to disciple folks until they themselves mature in Christ and are able to fend for themselves. Of course, to teach, you must have been taught, and moreover to be taught you must avail yourself to authority/help and be open for change.

Who are you feeding Fam.? We all have work to do. Jesus said "feed my sheep".

I'm jus sayin...Luv me.

***

Good morning Fam.. Continuing on this weeks theme, "feed my sheep", "being confident of this very thing, that He who has begun a good work in you will <u>complete it</u> until the day of Jesus Christ;" Phillippians 1:6

Fam God loves us so much that he wants only the best for us, His completed work. It is not enough for us to be saved. Salvation is just the beginning of the work.
Your spirit is saved the day you believe in your heart and confess with your mouth the lordship of Jesus. For your soul (mind, will and emotions) to be saved we must all go through "the process".

Nobody has a baby and just sets it out to grow and develop on its own. It needs nurturing. The same goes and even more so in the spiritual world. People have been misinformed by lazy preachers and evangelists to believe that once you are saved your life becomes a rose garden. It's assumed that upon salvation you automatically lose all desires to fulfill the lusts you had before you got saved. Something must be wrong when bad thoughts pop up, so you must get saved again and again.

THIS IS WHAT I CALL STINKIN THINKIN. My salvation is not based on my performance, how good or bad I am. My salvation is based on my faith in the Word, which says that if I believe, repent and confess I will be saved. However, for God to finish the work He started I must cooperate by partaking of His word, continuing in fellowship with other Christians, submitting to authority and being fed and nurtured in the Word.

For you who are mature in the Word, your job is to help nurture the new converts, "feed His sheep." For you who are new to this salvation thing, avail yourself to teaching and prepare to go through "the process", it ain't easy, but it's worth it.

I'm jus sayin...Luv me.

***

Good morning Fam.. Jesus said, "Feed my Sheep". Finishing up on this week's theme, I would like to submit to you what we are to feed His sheep. The Word says, "man shall not live by bread alone, but every word proceeding from the mouth of God".

This tells me that my survival in the Kingdom of God depends on my diet, not my physical diet, but my spiritual diet. For so many years many churches have fed sheep holy sounding quotes, fancy words that sound like they could be scripture and even lines from popular gospel songs that sound empowering. Example: for a long time, I thought "God blesses the child that has his own" was scripture, how absurd. As a result of this when trials and tribulations come many have turned away from God because they have not been rooted and grounded in the authentic, life giving and powerful Word of God.

"For the word of God is living and powerful, and sharper than any two-edged sword, piercing even to the division of soul and spirit, and of joints and marrow, and is a discerner of the thoughts and intents of the heart." Hebrews 4:12
In the end, only the word can keep you, it is the power of God, it is God.
"In the beginning was the Word, and the Word was with God, and the Word was God." John 1:1

When we break the bread of life with "His Sheep", we are imparting the Rhema (living word, life giving word) substance of

God, and that my friends will give anyone who receives it staying power, enabling "His sheep" to stand in the midst of storms.

 I'm jus sayin...Luv me.

***

Good morning and TGIF Fam.. "Feed My Sheep" has been a good study this week. I thank God for placing it on my heart to share. I pray that it has given you a new resolve to share the gospel with babes in Christ. "Are you your brother's keeper"? In the Kingdom of God, the answer is a resounding YES. "Feed my sheep" was not a request from Christ, it was a command. Every believer shares in the responsibility to raise the babies in Christ.

I'm reminded of a saying that we shared as younguns in Harambee 360, an experimental theater I was involved in. That saying was," If you don't know, learn. If you know, teach". If people in the world can do that, how much more do you think the people of God should practice this principle?
The Kingdom of God is marching to new heights and "church as we knew it" is no longer acceptable. As a matter of fact the Word says that you are the church, not just some building you go to. The work of the Lord is moving outside of the church building walls. We must adapt to be flexible enough to share what "thus says the Lord". This pleases God.
When two or more are gathered together in His name (just talking about Him), He is in the midst. Imagine that. You and another sharing about the good news of what God has done, and He's standing right there in your midst! That thought from His Word gives me the warm and fuzzies

As I do every week at this time, I ask, no beg of you to find a body of bible believing believers to join in offering God some corporate praise. There, you can flourish and grow together.

I'm jus sayin...Luv me.

***

Good morning Fam.. "Trust in the Lord with all **your** heart, And **lean not on your own understanding**; In all **your** ways acknowledge Him, And He shall direct **your** paths". <u>Proverbs 3:5-6</u>

Greetings and salutations to you on this fine Monday. I declare over you today, all of the best that God has to offer. I decree that should you decide to trust in Him and lean not to your own understanding, He will direct your paths and perform all of the promises that you take from His word, in due season.

Speak life to your own situation. Choose to guard the very words from your mouth. Use them to be a creative force of change for your own betterment. In other words, prophecy life, good health, peace, and wholeness into existence by using your own tongue as a creative force for good.
"For we walk by faith, not by sight". Faith in the finished work of Christ, not the futility of what we see. "For our light affliction, which is but for a moment, is working for us a far more exceeding *and* eternal weight of glory, while we do not look at the things which are seen, but at the things which are not seen. For the things which are seen *are* temporary, but the things which are not seen *are* eternal." 2 Corinthians 4:17-18

All that we see is temporary (it shall pass), what we do not see is eternal. Today I choose to believe the report of the Lord for my life, my future, my family and my friends. The lies of the enemy I will not even entertain.
God is doing some awesome things in the earth and also in and through His people, but it is up to us to choose His way or our own.

I'm jus sayin...Luv me.

***

Good morning Fam.. I was terribly disheartened recently when religion reared its ugly head during one of my daily posts. When I say religion I mean doctrines of men, silly rules and restrictions that a certain church sets, that has nothing to do with the Word.

Sadly many have been misled by leaders that "have a form of godliness, but deny the fullness of its power". 2 Timothy 3:5 says, "And from such people turn away!"

Man will attempt to complicate what God has simplified. Making it difficult for folks to come to a Christ, Who says "Take My yoke upon you and learn from Me, for I am gentle and lowly in heart, and you will find rest for your souls. For My yoke *is* easy and My burden is light." Matthew 11:29-30
The enemy will make it seem like you have to jump through hoops to achieve salvation when Romans 10:9-10 says "that if you confess with your mouth the Lord Jesus and believe in your heart that God has raised Him from the dead, you will be saved."
Let's not get it twisted, there will be growth and maturing required after anyone makes a commitment to follow Christ. Sometimes folks are not willing to change from their old ways, or repent. It's been said that change is the hardest thing for a man to do. However, in Him and being led by the Holy Spirit (The Comforter) that Jesus sent to guide, teach and lead us into all truth we die daily to our old man and become alive to Christ.

Come on Fam, let's keep it simple. Trust the Word! Study it to know for yourselves so that men will not be able to deceive you.

I'm jus sayin...Luv me.

***

Good morning Fam.. Every now and then we have to come clean before the Lord (prayerfully daily). Today I'm posting such a prayer from the psalmist David, Psalm 51 from the message bible. I don't know who (besides me) can use this, but I pray it helps someone.

David was called a man after God's own heart and prayers like these made him chosen.

"Generous in love—God, give grace! Huge in mercy—wipe out my bad record.
Scrub away my guilt, soak out my sins in your laundry. I know how bad I've been; my sins are staring me down.
You're the One I've violated, and you've seen it all, seen the full extent of my evil. You have all the facts before you; whatever you decide about me is fair.
I've been out of step with you for a long time, in the wrong since before I was born. What you're after is truth from the inside out. Enter me, then; conceive a new, true life.
Soak me in your laundry and I'll come out clean, scrub me and I'll have a snow-white life. Tune me into foot-tapping songs, set these once-broken bones to dancing. Don't look too close for blemishes, give me a clean bill of health.
God, make a fresh start in me, shape a Genesis week from the chaos of my life.
Don't throw me out with the trash, or fail to breathe holiness in me. Bring me back from gray exile, put a fresh wind in my sails! Give me a job teaching rebels your ways so the lost can find their way home.
Commute my death sentence, God, my salvation God, and I'll sing anthems to your life-giving ways. Unbutton my lips, dear God; I'll let loose with your praise."
Be Blessed Fam!

I'm jus sayin...Luv me.

***

Good morning Fam.. Blessings and peace be upon you, in the name, which is above all names, JESUS. Our God has been called by many names. Wars have been wages, churches divided and religious sects have been born based solely on what men insisted was the name of God.
However, if you've ever been in a car wreck who did you call on? Have you or a loved one ever made an announcement like, "I've been diagnosed with cancer"?. What name did you call on?

I don't care what or who you say you believe in, ninety-nine-point nine percent of the time during the time of a catastrophic event most people will call on "JESUS". I've never ever heard anyone call Buddha, Allah or any other god during times when an instant resolution is required. There is power, healing, deliverance, salvation, etcetera, etcetera to the infinity in the name, "JESUS".

This week we will be going down a road entitled, "Just Who Is God". In the meanwhile, try calling that name "JESUS" when you are alone, riding in your car, at home, at work, sitting at your desk, etcetera. There truly is something about that name that can change circumstances. Try it for yourself, it works.
I'm jus sayin...Luv me.

***

Good morning Fam.. It's time for the true body of Christ to stand together in unity, letting go of the petty differences that the enemy is using to divide the body. The old adage, divide and conquer has never been more prevalent than now. Many ministries instead of preaching what thus says the Lord, use their platform to tear down other pastors, ministries, ways people worship, and the list goes on and on. More focus should be on maturing the saints so that together we all can be declaring war on the works of the enemy.

When we, as the body of Christ, can grow up (mature) and be conjoined. Touching and agreeing against the works of the enemy, instead of pointing out every fault that we see in our brothers walk. We will be effective tools for evangelism, bringing many into the Kingdom of God, preparing the way for Jesus's return. Fam we(the body of Christ) need to let go of the petty jealousies, envies and silly arguments that don't profit the Kingdom. These divide us to keep us ineffective.

Ephesians 4:11-16 "And He Himself gave some to be apostles, some prophets, some evangelists, and some pastors and teachers, for the equipping of the saints for the work of ministry, for the edifying (building up, not tearing down) of the body of Christ, till we all come to the unity of the faith and of the knowledge of the Son of God, to a perfect man, to the measure of the stature of the fullness of Christ; that we should no longer be children, tossed to and fro and carried about with every wind of doctrine, by the trickery of men, in the cunning craftiness of deceitful plotting, but, speaking the truth in love, may grow up in all things into Him who is the head—Christ— from whom the whole body, joined and knit together by what every joint supplies, according to the effective working by which every part does its share, causes growth of the body for the edifying of itself in love". Ephesians 4:11-16

I don't know who this was for, but I do pray that I was hearing correctly, as I spoke what thus says the Lord, to my heart this morning.

I'm jus sayin...Luv me.

***

Good morning Fam.. "For the word of God is living and powerful, and sharper than any two-edged sword, piercing even to the division of soul and spirit, and of joints and marrow, and is a discerner of the thoughts and intents of the heart. And there is no creature hidden from His sight, but all things are naked and open to the eyes of Him to whom we must give account." Hebrews 4:12-13

The Message Bible puts it like this. "God means what he says. What he says goes. His powerful Word is sharp as a surgeon's scalpel, cutting through everything, whether doubt or defense, laying us open to listen and obey. Nothing and no one is impervious to God's Word. We can't get away from it—no matter what."

Yesterday we spoke on the urgent need for Christians to put aside differences and "be about our Father's business". Winning souls, saving lives, restoring folks, our ministry of reconciliation, reconciling the unsaved and backslidden to Christ. Righteous judgement begins in the house of God. However, I believe that our energies should be spent on reaching the lost at any cost, maturing and discipling new believers. If we focus on the hurting, starving, folks that are without hope, we won't have time to criticize others in the body of Christ that may not do everything exactly the way we do them.

The Word is living and powerful, nothing is hidden from It. Let it do its thing. Convicting, rebuking, and setting things straight. Let us stop trying to be the Holy Spirit for all men. Let God be God and let us do our part by bringing others into the kingdom.

I'm jus sayin...Luv me.

**

Good morning Fam..This morning I was moved by this description of JESUS in The Message Bible, all I can say is WOW.

Isaiah 53 "Who believes what we've heard and seen? Who would have thought God's saving power would look like this? The servant grew up before God—a scrawny seedling, a scrubby plant in a parched field. There was nothing attractive about him, nothing to cause us to take a second look. He was looked down on and passed over, a man who suffered, who knew pain firsthand. One look at him and people turned away. We looked down on him, thought he was scum. But the fact is, it was our pains he carried— our disfigurements, all the things wrong with us. We thought he brought it on himself, that God was punishing him for his own failures.
But it was our sins that did that to him, that ripped and tore and crushed him—our sins! He took the punishment, and that made us whole. Through his bruises we get healed. We're all like sheep who've wandered off and gotten lost. We've all done our own thing, gone our own way. And God has piled all our sins, everything we've done wrong, on him, on him.

He was beaten, he was tortured, but he didn't say a word. Like a lamb taken to be slaughtered and like a sheep being sheared, he took it all in silence. Justice miscarried, and he was led off—and did anyone really know what was happening? He died without a thought for his own welfare, beaten bloody for the sins of my people. They buried him with the wicked, threw him in a grave with a rich man, even though he'd never hurt a soul or said one word that wasn't true.

 Still, it's what God had in mind all along, to crush him with pain. The plan was that he give himself as an offering for sin so that he'd see life come from it—life, life, and more life. And God's plan will deeply prosper through him. Out of that terrible travail of soul, he'll see that it's worth it and be glad he did it. Through what he experienced, my righteous one, my servant, will make many "righteous ones," as he himself carries the burden of their sins." Therefore, I'll reward him extravagantly—the best of everything, the highest honors—Because he looked death in the face and didn't flinch, because he embraced the company of the lowest. He took on his own shoulders the sin of the many, he took up the cause of all the black sheep".

I pray that this Word has helped you, as it did me. To know that Jesus paid it all for me makes me appreciate Him even the more.

I'm jus sayin...Luv me.

***

Good morning Fam.. "If with heart and soul you're doing good, do you think you can be stopped? Even if you suffer for it, you're still better off. Don't give the opposition a second thought. Through thick and thin, keep your hearts at attention, in adoration before Christ, your Master. Be ready to speak up and tell anyone who asks why you're living the way you are, and always with the utmost courtesy. Keep a clear conscience before God so that when people throw mud at you, none of it will stick. They'll end up realizing that they're the ones who need a bath. It's better to suffer for doing good, if that's what God wants, than to be punished for doing bad. That's what Christ did definitively: suffered because of others' sins, the Righteous One for the unrighteous ones. He went through it all—was put to death and then made alive—to bring us to God."
1 Peter 3:18 MSG

I am so glad today to be serving an I AM God, not an I was god or an I will be god. I don't have to rely solely on my memories of what He has done for me, which has been so much that a book cannot contain it. Nor do I have to relate solely to what I, by faith, believe that God is going to do for me. My eyes have not seen nor has it entered into my heart the plans that God has for me. However, today I can say that I am serving the I AM GOD, who is a present help in the times of trouble, answering me even before I call upon Him. Making sure that my calling is sure.

Stay tuned this week we will discuss the I AM God and the benefit of serving Him now.
I'm jus sayin...Luv me.

***

Good morning Fam.."In the beginning GOD created the heavens and the earth." Gen.1:1

God-Elohim, most high God, strong one, father, alpha, sovereign one, creator, author. These are all attributes of the God we serve. Our verse today speaks of God creating the heavens and earth. We will learn by reading further that He did it by speaking it into existence.

If we have been born again, we, who were born in sin naturally become the sons of God. We're grafted into His bloodline by receiving the salvation freely given and by us accepting the finished work of Jesus Christ on Calvary's cross. This one act of salvation gives us the DNA of our new daddy, God. Having one's DNA causes us to, whether we know this person or not, act like, look like and share the characteristics of the person.

(SIDEBAR)Personally I never met my natural dad until I turned 21 years old, but upon meeting him, found out that we were similar in many ways.

When we become God's son, John 1:12 says, "But as many as received him, to them gave he power to become the sons of God, even to them that believe on his name:" He gives us the POWER to share in His attributes and in giving us that, we have the power to create our future with our words. God, in creation, only spoke what he wanted to see and He then said, "It is good".

Fam I submit to you today if you belong to Elohim, you have that same ability. Sadly however, many of us would rather speak on our problems, circumstances, obstacles and challenges, elevating them.

Choose to speak only on what you hope to see and watch God perform it. As my Pastor would say, "your future or your funeral is in your tongue".

I'm jus sayin...Luv me.

***

Good morning Fam.."And Moses said unto God, Behold, when I come unto the children of Israel, and shall say unto them, The God of your fathers hath sent me unto you; and they shall say to me, what is his name? what shall I say unto them? God said unto Moses, I AM THAT I AM: and he said, Thus shalt thou say unto the children of Israel, I AM hath sent me unto you." Exodus 3:13-14

Fam, right now in your own personal life is God the I AM God to you? Could he be the God of I was because you remember things

He's done for you or a family member? Or maybe you hope to have God show up strong in your life and He's the I will be God! I heard the words "you're gonna die tonight, we are gonna kill you tonight fats". Even though I was in a backslidden state, reprobate in mind and knew that I had gone far from God. The I AM God showed up. My response to my attackers was, "I don't think so". Although I was outnumbered six to one, somehow I knew in my spirit that God wasn't quite finished with me yet. There was still more work for me to do, these guys couldn't kill me today!
The I AM God provided for me a way of escape (I was bloodied, but I survived).

Backslidden in a state of having a seared conscience and a practicing junkie, I once lived on five bags or shots of heroin a day. A fellow junkie who was a half partner(one who splits the cost on a bag when you can't afford the whole thing) that particular day asked "what is it with you, you always treat me fair and never try to cheat me". By then the dope we had just shot together was taking effect. In the midst of taking a nod (the dope was good) I told him, "for real I'm a Christian and I know that one day I'll have to go return to God".
Fam although I've walked away from God more than once, (don't try this at home, for it may end in death) He has always had His hands on me. I can't explain why He has toiled with me even when I cursed Him, but I am so glad He did. I AM THAT I AM has always seen me through.

When I AM got tired of watching me suffer at my own hands and wanted to get my attention bad enough, off to jail or penitentiary I would go. Somehow when all the inmates go to sleep and the lights go out, God speaks the loudest! I couldn't hear God while running the streets, working on surviving, but being in a cage calms the savage beasts and opens their ears.

It may seem strange to you, but I must admit, I've never been arrested, only rescued!
I'm jus sayin...Luv me.

***

Good morning Fam.. "Blessed is the man Who walks not in the counsel of the ungodly, Nor stands in the path of sinners, Nor sits in the seat of the scornful; But his delight is in the law of the LORD, And in His law he meditates day and night". "He shall be like a tree Planted by the rivers of water, that brings forth its fruit in its season, whose leaf also shall not wither; And whatever he does shall prosper.

The ungodly are not so, But are like the chaff which the wind drives away. Therefore, the ungodly shall not stand in the judgment, Nor sinners in the congregation of the righteous. For the LORD knows the way of the righteous, But the way of the ungodly shall perish". Psalm 1
David, in Psalm one wrote a very clear formula for being blessed. The formula is so simple that many cannot follow it.

His number one point is that we as Christians do not receive or walk in the counsel of those who do not know God. Many times I have seen on these pages, folks getting counseling from folks who have no idea of who God is. It's like the old adage, the blind leading the blind. Counsel from a fool (fool-one who refuses to acknowledge God) will make the one receiving counsel a fool.

We will be exploring this Psalm in depth this week, but in the meantime chew on and digest this first installation.

Who are you receiving counsel from?

I'm jus sayin...Luv me.

***

Good morning Fam..I know I promised to explore Psalm 1 this week, but in light of the holiday excuse me if I take a sidebar and return to that next week.

The world has set aside a day during the year that we are to give thanks for our many blessings. Many will eat, drink and be merry while taking a momentary break to thank God for the food and family time. That for many is good. However, my prayer for all of us is that we not only give thanks on Thanksgiving Day but it becomes a part of our daily lifestyle. All men ought to be giving thanks at every opportunity we get.

I don't know about you, but the life that I've lived and things He has brought me through cause me to give thanks at every thought of His goodness. God didn't have to bring me through any of the situations I've put myself in, but He did. Therefore, I'm thankful in my spirit and my soul thanks God for life itself. I may not have everything I want. I may not have achieved all the things that I want to achieve, yet I am thankful for another day and another chance to get it right, every day that I awaken.

Just a few scriptures that might help us to be thankful every day, and not just on Thanksgiving.
Psalm 95:2 "Let us come before His presence with thanksgiving; Let us shout joyfully to Him with psalms."

Psalm 100:4 "Enter into His gates with thanksgiving, And into His courts with praise. Be thankful to Him, and bless His name."

Eph 5:20 "giving thanks always for all things to God the Father in the name of our Lord Jesus Christ"

Fam I submit to you, everyday should be Thanksgiving.

I'm jus sayin...Luv me.

***

Good morning Fam..Back to this week's subject, David's keys to being blessed. Based in Psalm 1.

Verses 1-2, "Blessed is the man Who walks not in the counsel of the ungodly, Nor stands in the path of sinners, Nor sits in the seat of the scornful, but his delight is in the law of the LORD, And in His law he meditates day and night."
We established the fact Monday that if we as Christians seek counsel from men who deny God) we too ourselves become fools, like the blind leading the blind, they both fall in the ditch they cannot see.

Standing in the path of sinners is to me self-explanatory. Just as A.A. or N.A (Alcoholics Anonymous and Narcotics Anonymous) teaches, sometimes we have to change our people, places and things if we want true change. As hard as it may seem, sometimes folks from your troubled past you have to let go. I've said it earlier in the book and it's still true. "If you go to the barbershop enough, whether you want it or not, sooner or later you're gonna get a haircut."

Next in line is "sitting in the seat of the scornful". A scornful person is one who holds on to scorn. They've been rejected, someone has wronged them(in their minds anyway). Maybe they weren't chosen for a position they thought they were qualified for and one or more of these actions has made them bitter. I know this one oh too well and have to constantly ask the Lord to keep me in check.

From a young age, I have often felt overlooked and passed over for positions or things I felt I could have done a far better job at, than the person chosen. I finally came to a place in life where I accepted the fact that what God has for me is for me, no one else can have it.

A scornful person can't help but talk about his or her scorn and aligning with others who don't mind talking about it. This is a dangerous place, as it leads to envies and jealousies. Don't go there and if you find yourself there, REPENT NOW.

Closing for today with, "But his delight is in the law of the LORD, And in His law he meditates day and night". He shall be like a tree Planted by the rivers of water, brings forth its fruit in its season, Whose leaf also shall not wither; And whatever he does shall prosper."

And whatsoever he DOES shall prosper. God can't bless it unless you do it. God cannot bless what we will not do. We cannot think it, wish it or dream it, but we must DO IT. We grossly underestimate the effort needed to get something done. When it doesn't come easily we just quit, thinking God isn't in it.
Fam when we delight ourselves in the law of the Lord, meditate on His word and find our pleasure in Him, WE WILL BE BLESSED.

Let that marinate in your spirit, have a happy Thanksgiving and I'll see you Friday.

I'm jus sayin...Luv me.

***

Good morning Fam..We will finish the study we started last week on David's keys to being blessed based on Psalm 1. For any who missed any of it I would suggest that you go back on my page to last Monday. Read the posts and I am sure you will be blessed by this study.

Picking up where we left off let's go to Psalm 1:2-3 "But his delight is in the law of the Lord, in His law he meditates day and night. He shall be like a tree. Planted by the rivers of water. That brings forth its fruit in its season. Whose leaf also shall not wither; AND WHATEVER HE DOES SHALL PROSPER."

In summation of the whole of Psalm 1. The Word says, and I put it in CAPS to make it shout to you. The man who follows this recipe.

1.walking not in ungodly counsel
2. standing in sinners paths
3. does not sit in seats with scornful folks
4. delights himself in the law of the Lord
5. and meditates on it day and night.

*That man will be like a tree with deep roots that are constantly watered, because he is by the "rivers of water".
*That man shall also abound with fruitfulness as he obeys God's command to "be fruitful and multiply".
*His leaves (source of nourishment) also shall not wither.
*AND (I really like this part and pray that you get it) "WHATEVER HE DOES SHALL PROSPER".

Fam it is God's will for you to prosper, and prosperity is not only measured in dollars and cents. There are formulas or instructions written in His Word to prepare us for and direct us to prosperity. God has so much more for us than many churches (temples of religion, not relationship) teach. He doesn't want us to have to wait on "pie in the sky in the great by and by". It is His desire for us to have heaven right here on earth. It's all about our choices.

My God this is getting good!

I'm jus sayin...Luv me.

***

Good morning Fam.. Does it seem sometimes like all hell is breaking out around you? Has your job security, friends, the things you once felt comfortable with all of a sudden changed? Does it seem like you are under attack from Satan himself and the heat has turned up to almost unbearable degrees?

WELL, GET TO PRAISING GOD!! There is a shift going on in the atmosphere and for many of us this shift feels uncomfortable.

REJOICE!! God is moving many of us out of our comfort zones to take us to a new place. The Word of God says "the eyes have not seen, nor ears heard, neither has it entered into the heart of man, the things God has prepared for those who love Him."
1 Corinthians 2:9

GOD IS DOING A NEW THING, the time spoken of in the bible when God's people will receive the riches of the evil, will live in houses that they did not build, will receive promotions, businesses, and favor that the world cannot understand, are upon us.

However, you must understand that diamonds are not formed without intense pressure. Gold is brought forth after enduring intense heat. Cake mix is no good unless it's put under the fire.

FAINT NOT under what seems like the enemies attack, many times it's not the enemy at all but God's incubation period for you.

Like the Hebrew boys Shadrach, Meschak and Abednigo, if we praise God while in the furnace, he will join us and we will come out of the fire, not only unscorched , not smelling like smoke, but we will come out as pure gold.
SO DON'T TRIP WHEN THE HEAT TURNS UP!

I'm jus sayin...Luv me.

***

Good morning Fam.. "Do not remember the former things, Nor consider the things of old. Behold, I will do a new thing, Now it shall spring forth; Shall you not know it?
I will even make a road in the wilderness And rivers in the desert."
Isaiah 43:18-19

Concerning the hard times you are facing. The Lord is saying "fear not, if you are His, He's got you. He has not forgotten you, you are not alone. Although it seems that everyone has turned their backs on you, He is more than them. He is THE GREAT I AM."

"But now, thus says the LORD, who created you, O Jacob,And He who formed you, O Israel:
" Fear not, for I have redeemed you; I have called you by your name; You are Mine.
When you pass through the waters, I will be with you; And through the rivers, they shall not overflow you.
When you walk through the fire, you shall not be burned, Nor shall the flame scorch you.
For I am the LORD your God, The Holy One of Israel, your Savior;
I gave Egypt for your ransom, Ethiopia and Seba in your place.
Since you were precious in My sight, You have been

honored, And I have loved you;
Therefore I will give men for you, And people for your life.
Fear not, for I am with you; I will bring your descendants from the east and gather you from the west;
I will say to the north, 'Give them up!' And to the south, 'Do not keep them back!'
Bring My sons from afar, And My daughters from the ends of the earth—
Everyone who is called by My name, Whom I have created for My glory;
I have formed him, yes, I have made him."
Isaiah 43:1-7

He's jus sayin...Luv me.

***

Good morning and TGIF Fam.. Great is the Lord and greatly to be praised! I believe the Lord has really spoken to many hearts this week through these posts. If you missed any, please scroll backwards on my page to read for yourselves what was shared.

As I do on Fridays of most weeks, I ask you, no beg of you to join with some other believers who rightly divide the Word of God to offer Him some corporate praise. He inhabits the praises of His people and there is absolutely nothing that compares to being in His presence. Yokes are broken, people are set free and His people can soak in the essence of all that He is. If you don't know of such a place to join with others please feel free to inbox me and I'll share with you, "My Safe Place".

I'm jus sayin...Luv me.

***

Good morning Fam.. It is a glorious Monday. It's a great day to be alive. In spite of the fact that the world curses this day as one that is not so desirable because it is the first day of the work week.

"This is the day which the Lord has made; We will rejoice and be glad in it." Psalm 118:24

I believe in my heart of hearts that David was writing about Mondays when he penned those words.

We as Christians have to get to the point where we take a stand and stop conforming to the world's way of thinking and talking. How can anyone who has accepted Christ in their hearts call anything that God has created accursed? That is, in effect, cursing what God has blessed.

"And do not be conformed to this world, but be transformed by the renewing of your mind, that you may prove what is that good and acceptable and perfect will of God." Romans 12:2

Fam instead of the church being transformed into the image of a loving God. We are busy being conformed into the image of the world that hates God. We want to dress like them, talk like them and make sure that we keep up with the latest trends even if that means speaking curses on things that God has blessed.

"Death and life are in the power of the tongue, And those who love it will eat its fruit." Proverbs 18:21

Your tongue is the author of the fruit you will eat. You can speak life and blessings into your life or curses and death. It's on you to choose.

I'm jus sayin...Luv me.

***

Good morning Fam.. Blessed be the name of the Lord and blessed are they that hear Him.

Today I feel led to share The Word as written in Proverbs, known as the book of wisdom. These scriptures truly need no explanation, they speak for themselves.

"Then they will call on me, but I will not answer; will seek me diligently, but they will not find me.
Because they hated knowledge And did not choose the fear of the LORD, They would have none of my counsel, And despised my every rebuke.
Therefore, they shall eat the fruit of their own way, And be filled to the full with their own fancies.
For the turning away of the simple will slay them, And the complacency of fools will destroy them;" Prov.1:28-32

Just a few more random thoughts that jumped off the pages, enjoy.

"The fear of the LORD is the beginning of knowledge, But fools despise wisdom and instruction."

"The way of a fool is right in his own eyes, but he who heeds counsel is wise."

"Good understanding gains favor, But the way of the unfaithful is hard"

Thus says the Lord!

I'm jus sayin...Luv me.

***

Good morning Fam.. "But seek first the kingdom of God and His righteousness, and all these things shall be added to you."

Fam the greatest statement I could leave with you for this weekend and the rest of your life is "seek first the Kingdom of God and all the things you desire will be added to you" Matt 6:33

We as a people seek many things, love, partners, careers, finances, material things, etcetera, etcetera, etcetera. The people who have many of these things already find that after acquiring things, they are still not happy.

Every man/woman alive has an empty space in their souls (soul-mind, will, emotions) unless it is filled with Jesus, they find that there is something missing. Therefore, they spend a lifetime trying to get more, or the next thing that they think will make them happy.

Many millionaires have committed suicide because after they get all the toys, money, houses and relationships they find that they are still not satisfied. Why? Because this hole in the soul I speak of, can only be satisfied and righteously filled when we allow God to take His place in it.

If we in fact seek Him first, He will add the desires of our hearts to our life.

This weekend I ask you , no beg you to find a place to join with other believers who rightly divide the Word of God to join in offering God some corporate praise. He abides in the praises of

His people and in His presence is the fullness of joy. If you care to know where my "safe place of worship" is, inbox me.

I'm jus sayin...Luv me.

***

Good morning Fam.. Growing up we often made jokes about people and churches that we considered "holy and sanctified". That term had a certain mysterious connotation to it and for those of us who were not trained in the Word the term was scary, lol..
 I remember clearly as a child playing a game in which we'd chase each other around the house screaming hulee ghost (Holy Ghost), hulee ghost, hulee ghost. I didn't know then that the same "hulee ghost" we childishly feared as we ran from the person screaming it, was in fact the third part of the Godhead sent back by Jesus to be our comforter, teacher and guide. I didn't know that years later I would depend on that Holy Ghost to bring me into all truths and guide me through some dangerous situations. Better yet, the same Holy Ghost would speak assurances of God's guidance to me when I felt God had left or abandoned me.

We also used to make snide remarks about "those sanctified folks", having no understanding of the word sanctified (set apart by God for a purpose). We understood even less that sanctification was a process that is ongoing, not instant. Sanctification is in fact progressive in nature. Many have been taught erroneously that it is instant.

Also, some say the moment you accept Jesus you are instantly perfect(NOT). If you are not, maybe your salvation didn't take, and just maybe there is something wrong with you. WRONG!!!!

When we accept Christ in our hearts the process is only starting. When we are "born again" it is just as being born in the natural world. As a baby no one walks and talks instantly. There is a process that needs to take place.

As a babe in Christ, you need to be fed the milk of the Word.

"as newborn babes, desire **the** pure **milk of the word**, that you may grow **the**reby," 1 Peter 2:2

"For everyone who partakes *only* **of milk** *is* unskilled in **the word of** righteousness, for he is a babe". Hebrews 5:13
You don't come from the womb mature and ready for the world, and neither do you as a babe in Christ.

Gotta go now but it seems that this is a subject that may require a few days, stick with me. I think that God is about to open some eyes this week and dispel many falsehoods we have been taught. I'm excited!
I'm jus sayin...Luv me.

***

Good morning Fam.. We started this week speaking on how as a kid we joked about and made fun of people we thought were "holy and sanctified". Ignorance of a thing can and will cause folks to fear it, make fun of it and overall misunderstand its importance.

How could I have known as a child that the Holy Ghost would be my teacher, comforter and guide, the one Jesus promised when He announced His departure? How could I have known that Jehovah-Mekoddishkem (the Lord my sanctifier) only wants to consecrate, cleanse, purify and set me and you apart for our purpose in life.

Sanctification is not something to be ashamed of or fear. Sanctification is something to be desired. Just as new Christians are to desire the sincere milk of the Word.

Sanctification is also not an instantaneous event that happens the moment that we are saved. If you have accepted Christ and have stumbled, made a ton of mistakes, or even revisited an old sin, you don't have to be saved again. There is nothing wrong with you, nothing that the renewing of the mind by washing it with the Word will not handle. Get the Word in you. The more Word in you, the less you'll have a propensity to sin. There's a saying that goes. "Sin will keep you from the Word and the Word will keep you from sin".

"So shall My word be that goes forth from My mouth; It shall not return to Me void, But it shall accomplish what I please, And it shall prosper in the thing for which I sent it." Isaiah 55:11

Fam I conclude on that note from the Word. If we get it in us, sin will diminish in us. Not overnight, but it's an ongoing process that comes with many knee scrapes, stumbles and falls.

I'm jus sayin...Luv me.

***

Good morning Fam.. I feel led to deviate from this week's subject. A friend of mine brought up a subject last night that moved me to be cognizant of a fact.

Fact is, we all must be aware that no day nor hour is promised to any of us. We must take serious our relationship or non-relationship with Christ. I'm not talking about going to a building (church) once a week. I am talking about you being sure that if you died today, you would be with Him.

"For God so loved the world that He gave His only begotten Son, that whoever believes in Him should not perish but have everlasting life." John 3:16

Whenever the scripture talks about perishing. It is speaking about eternal separation from God. In layman's terms, going to hell. Church membership, good works, being a good person, treating everybody right and living a "good life" does not ensure that we will spend eternity with God. Many have gone to hell after completing all of these worldly tests and passing with flying colors.

Romans 10:9-10 says "that if you confess with your mouth the Lord Jesus and believe in your heart that God has raised Him from the dead, you will be saved. For with the heart one believes unto righteousness, and with the mouth confession is made unto salvation."

Please, if you think you have not confessed Jesus, say the following prayer out loud today. Make sure that if you die you will spend eternity with God.

Jesus, I come to you today realizing that I have sinned and come short of You in my life. I ask You to forgive me of my sins today. I believe that You are the Son of God. I believe that You died to pay for my sins. I accept your finished work on Calvary's cross as I give my life to You today. Be my guide from this day forth. Speak to my heart by Your precious Holy Spirit. Give me a hunger for Your Word and shape my will to conform to what Your Word says. I thank You for salvation. I receive it by faith. In the name of Jesus, I pray…Amen.

I'm jus sayin...Luv me.

***

Good morning and TGIF Fam.." My soul magnifies the Lord, my spirit has rejoiced in God my Savior. For He who is mighty has done great things for me, holy is His name."(Luke 1:46-47,49)

This week the topic has been on how we as kids made fun of, feared and even mocked those that we thought were "holy and sanctified." The point was made that we as humans often fear, misunderstand, and make fun of things that we don't have knowledge or are ignorant of.

Holy is defined simply as, set apart for the worship of God. Holy doesn't signify that you are perfect, (we fall down, but we get up). We are to strive for, aspire to achieve, and work towards the goal of perfection in God. This attribute is described in the Word simply as a person who can control his or her tongue. Controlling your tongue, as you are led by the Spirit. Knowing what to say and when to say it. That is not such a bad idea, huh Fam.?

"My brethren, let not many of you become teachers, knowing that we shall receive a stricter judgment. For we all stumble in many things. If anyone does not stumble in word, he *is* a perfect man, able also to bridle the whole body". James 3:1-2

"Therefore gird up the loins of your mind, be sober, and rest your hope fully upon the grace that is to be brought to you at the revelation of Jesus Christ; as obedient children, not conforming yourselves to the former lusts, as in your ignorance; but as He who called you is holy, you also be holy in all your conduct, because it is written, "Be holy, for I am holy."1 Peter 1:13-16

I believe the Lord has called me. How about you? Has He put out a call on your life? Well if he has, He has also set you apart for the purpose of worshiping Him, sanctified you. You are holy and sanctified. What is wrong with that?

Be Blessed this weekend and find a place where people rightfully divide the Word, to join with in offering God some corporate praise. He inhabits the praises of His people.

I'm jus sayin...Luv me.

***

Good morning FB Fam.. "Let this mind be in you which was also in Christ Jesus, who, being in the form of God, did not consider it robbery to be equal with God, but made Himself of no reputation, taking the form of a servant and coming in the likeness of men." Phillipians 2:5-7

"Yet it shall not be so among you; but whoever desires to become great among you, let him be your servant. And whoever desires to

be first among you, let him be your slave—just as the Son of Man did not come to be served, but to serve, and to give His life a ransom for many." Matthew 20:26-28

Most of us secretly and some openly think that we want to sit at the highest seats. We quietly want to receive the glory that we perceive should come to our leaders in ministry. The question that begs to be asked is, are we willing to be a servant to all? Somehow we have gotten it twisted, observing Pastors who so willingly lay back and get waited on hand and foot. We see everyone lavishing compliments and gifts on them. Then we assume that leaders are to be served and not allowed to be servants.

Yes, we are to honor those who work hard to shepherd us, teach us, and bring us the Word of God week after week. However, written in Matthew are the words proceeding from Jesus's mouth that tell us, if you want to be great you must become "the slave", a servant to all. On top of that the Word says we must have the same mind in us that Jesus had.

I guess this word today was designed for any aspiring or current leaders and also for us who choose in the natural, whom we will follow. A leader who is not first a servant is not worthy to lead. If you want to lead Fam., get your serving up. Become a slave for the people of God.

Humble yourself in the sight of the Lord and in due season He will exalt you.

I'm jus sayin...Luv me.

***

Good morning Fam.. Bless the Lord on this fine Monday morning. This weekend was so blessed that my cup is truly running over. I believe it's going to run over on all of you who read these posts this week. The highlight of this weekend was a sermon by my Pastor, who broke down the twenty third Psalm like I've never heard it and with so much power that I believe it's going to jump from these pages this week.

I intend to share what I gleaned this week. Stay with me, it's going to be good. For today however, I will give you the Message Bible's version on Psalm 23, it speaks volumes and opens up this Psalm to your spiritual eyes like the King James version never did.

"God, my shepherd! I don't need a thing. You have bedded me down in lushness. You find me quiet pools to drink from. True to your word, you let me catch my breath and send me in the right direction.
Even when the way goes through Death Valley, I'm not

afraid when you walk at my side. Your trusty shepherd's
crook makes me feel secure. You serve me a six-course
dinner right in front of my enemies. You revive my drooping
head; my cup brims with blessing. Your beauty and love chase
after me every day of my life. I'm back home in the house
of God for the rest of my life."

This is going to be a good week. I prophesy over your lives right
now. God wants to bless you like never before and show you that
it was His goodness and mercy that has followed you all the days
of your lives.

I'm jus sayin...Luv me.

***

Good morning Fam..As I said yesterday, the highlight of my great
weekend was when Pastor broke down Psalm 23 like I've never
heard it before. As promised, I will attempt to share some of what
I gleaned from this message and I pray it helps you.

"The LORD is my shepherd (Pastor, leader, one appointed to
guide, look out for your safety by teaching you of possible pitfalls
and ruts in the road of life. He also instructs you in righteousness
so that you can make right choices); I shall not want(I don't want
because I am either fully supplied, or I know that my needs are
met by faith because I do what I'm supposed to do. Sow
financially into sound ministries, give offerings elsewhere, plant
seeds expecting a harvest. I also have been taught that I am a
Kings kid, heir to the throne and have an inheritance in God).

He makes me to lie down in green pastures (He leads his people to
places where they can be fed abundantly, above and beyond their
needs, more than enough); He leads me beside the still waters (the
still waters are where his sheep can drink to the full, be totally

satisfied. Still waters can be deep and troubled but on the surface they are calm with no sign of the danger that is lurking below. Some Christians are like that, there may be all hell breaking out in their lives and because of their relationship with and faith in their God, you would never be able to tell it by observing them. On the other hand there are Christians who are so shallow, you know every trouble they encounter. They are not shy about running and telling, they speak more about the issue than the solver of all issues. Their focus is not on the God who can and has delivered them. They can only see the trouble that is right before them and therefore speak on it).

Gotta stop now Fam., but tune in tomorrow. I believe it's getting good and gonna get better.

I'm jus sayin...Luv me.

***

Good morning Fam..Today we start on verse 3 of Psalm 23 as I give you my take on Pastor's Sunday sermon, let's get right to it.

Verse 3 "He restores my soul"

When something has been restored, it usually has gone through a certain amount of wearing out, abuse, weathering, dilapidation and rusting out. Your soul consists of your mind, will and emotions. The central part of you that controls everything that you do. Also, it governs how you make decisions and is the source of how you act or react.

I don't know about you, but when I came to Jesus and accepted Him as my own, my soul had to be restored. My mind had a way of dealing with situations that was nothing like what Jesus would do. Anyone calling themselves a Christian, must be Christlike. My will had to go through a transformation. As I grew up I was determined to do things my way, I worked, hustled and conned my way through my teenage years. Intent on making my own way. I was determined to not ask anybody for anything. My emotions were wrecked! I was a product of rejection from the womb, and rejection followed me. Growing up a fat kid, I was always the last chosen or sometimes not even chosen at all. All of this damages a person and leaves scars in their soul. These scars can only be wiped out as Christ "restores the soul", with the washing of the Word, renewing the mind and transforming power of the Holy Ghost.

"He leads me in the paths of righteousness For His name's sake."

God leads us in the way of Him. Many think that to be righteous we are without problems, faults, never making mistakes, SINLESS and above reproach. However, the verse implies that God leads us in the paths of righteousness, He takes us on paths that lead us to be in and with Him.

I submit to you today that this path is a lifelong journey from glory to glory. Nobody I know has ARRIVED. All of the real Christians I know will admit that God is still working on them. It's a process, sometimes painful, but worth every tear, every heartache, every battle and like the psalmist would say, "each victory will help you, some other to win".

I'm jus sayin...Luv me.

***

Good morning Fam..This week we have been breaking down and dissecting Psalm 23, inspired by the sermon I heard this past Sunday. In the beginning it was only what I had gleaned from hearing that sermon, but the Holy Ghost has expanded this thing and opened it up even more. If you have not been with me go back on my page through Monday, and catch some of the precious nuggets of living Word.

Verse 4 "Yea, though I walk through the valley of the shadow of death, I will fear no evil; For You are with me; Your rod and Your staff, they comfort me."

In order for the shadow of anything to fall on you, you must come close to it. I don't know about any of you, but I have surely come close to death many times. Sometimes I knew about it and sometimes I didn't. During the days when I was intent on killing myself (after my first wife's death). I had a saying, "yeah though I walk through the valley of the shadow of death, I will fear no evil, because I'm the baddest mother(forgive the allusion) in the valley". It was the drugs that caused me to have a false confidence in my ability to fight my way out of danger. I thought I was badd (yes double d bad) and I had many people around me fooled into believing that I was dangerous.

Looking back, when I came down from the highs of illegal drugs. I know that it was God's grace and mercy that followed me. He wasn't through with Don yet. He knew in the beginning of time that I would be writing these words to you today.

The place you are in right now, no matter how good or bad, is no surprise to God. His rod is an instrument used to stave off your possible attackers and His staff is used to save you from yourself. God has a plan for your life and even you cannot disrupt it. Take it from one who has tried, me. I have come to the place where I realize this and have given up on trying to fight His plan.

What about you? You can't win and you sure can't beat God.

I'm jus sayin...Luv me.

***

Good morning Fam.. This week's series on the breakdown of Psalm 23 has been so awesome, unfortunately there is too much material to finish today. We will finish next week, I promise.

Today I must pause to wish all of you a Merry and joyous Christmas.

This is the time that we celebrate the birth of the greatest gift of all, Jesus. Don't stop at telling the story of the baby in the manger, Emmanuel (God with us). Tell somebody about the good things He has done for you (the gospel). Share this free gift with whoever will listen.

In the spirit of Christmas help someone who is less fortunate than yourself. Proverbs 19:17 says "He who has pity on **the poor lends to the** Lord, And He will pay back what he has given". By helping the less fortunate you are helping Jesus Himself and there is no one that can pay you back like the giver of every good and perfect gift.

Christmas has become so commercialized that society has taken the emphasis off of Christ and put it all on the giving and receiving of gifts. However we must start a revolution of being Christlike at Christmas. We must be intentional about our efforts in helping someone less fortunate than ourselves. Try it and experience the joy of giving like never before.

I'm jus sayin...Luv me.

***

Good morning Fam..I do hope that your Christmases were all that you dreamed they would be and you were blessed beyond measure.

As promised, I will complete the exposition of Psalm 23 as we start this week. I think that this next verse was one of the best. It teaches us to appreciate our enemies.

VS 5 "You prepare a table before me in the presence of my enemies; You anoint my head with oil; My cup runs over." Regularly I see posts written by people who want to distance themselves from their haters or enemies. It is probably natural for folks to want to get rid of their enemies or haters. However, God's plan is contrary to popular attitudes in so many ways.

We see in this verse that He wants to prepare a table for you in the presence of your haters or enemies. Why? Nothing tastes better than a plate of your favorite foods eaten in front of those that don't want you to have it. I believe God does that so that they will know it was Him who has blessed you. Prayerfully your enemies will then turn towards the God you serve in repentance and desire to walk in the place of blessings that you are in.

Well time is up, see you tomorrow and I do hope that you were blessed by this abbreviated take on Psalm 23:5.

I'm jus sayin...Luv me.

***

Good morning Fam.. If you haven't been following this post since last Monday. You must treat yourself and go back on my page. Psalm 23:6 was so good that it might take us two days to finish. Let's get it done.

Psalm 23:6 "Surely goodness and mercy shall follow me all the days of my life; and I will dwell in the house of the Lord Forever."

In the beginning of this series we spoke of how our Father which is in heaven 1. makes me lie down in lush green pastures 2. leads me beside still waters 3. restores my soul (mind, will and emotions) 4. directs me in paths of righteousness, (to uphold His name). Because I trust in him I can and (personally), I have walked through valleys shadowed by death. Fearing no evil because His rod of correction and staff of protection comfort me. To cap this most quoted Psalm off is the fact that I am made aware that Goodness and Mercy will follow me ALL THE DAYS OF MY LIFE. I don't know about you, but when I look back on my life I know that I haven't always chosen to do the right thing. I sometimes put myself in some dangerous places where some would say I deserved the worst outcomes that could have befallen me. But when I look back, I now realize it was Goodness and Mercy following me through all of the days of MY life. GLORAAY!!!(that deserved a praise break)

Today I can say that I will dwell in the house of the Lord forever.

I'm jus sayin...Luv me.

***

Good morning Fam. I promise this is the last installation on the series that started last week when my Pastor opened up the twenty-third Psalm like I had never heard it before. I felt strongly in my spirit to share this word with you.

In the midst of sharing the Holy Spirit was allowed to have His way with the post. He took me outside of the boundaries of what I had gleaned, adding tidbits of wisdom. Let's finish and see what else God has for us.

Verse 6 take 2 "Surely goodness and mercy shall follow me All the days of my life; And I will dwell in the house of the LORD Forever."

Any one of you reading this post can think back in time and if you are honest, there were moments when you wondered "how did I make it through that". For me there was no doubt in my mind that "goodness and mercy" was following me. Grace allowed me to go through all of my backslidings, rebellions and moments of disobedience safe from any major physical or mental harm. It was also the grace of God that spared me from death. Many times, I've had my head in the lion's mouth, but it was Gods "goodness and mercy" that followed me.

My mind is now made up. Many good people that hear excerpts of my testimony literally beg me not to turn back again. My reply to them is basically, I don't have any more runs left in me. I have literally practiced running from God and He actually gave me a song to record about it titled "Run To You".

I am determined today to "dwell in the house of the Lord Forever".

Fam, I hope that in some small way this series has helped you.

I'm jus sayin...Luv me.

***

Good morning Fam.. "Let not your heart be troubled; you believe in God, believe also in Me. In My Father's house are many mansions; if it were not so, I would have told you. I go to prepare a place for you. And if I go and prepare a place for you, I will come again and receive you to Myself; that where I am, there you may be also. And where I go you know, and the way you know." John 14:1-4

In the bible these words are written in red, signifying they came from the Savior's mouth. They are pretty plain. Jesus is saying that He and His father are of one heart and one purpose, therefore we must believe in both.

Furthermore, Jesus is saying that He must leave this earth realm that we know of to prepare for us a place. The life that we know of is just for a moment, it is temporary. The true you is a spirit that lives eternally. Just as Jesus had to go and prepare a place for us, we have to prepare our souls and our spirits for the eternal.

We have a choice!

The wonderful thing about the God we serve is that He will not twist our arms, or otherwise force us to choose Him. "He is the way, the truth and the life" and will always put before us paths to take. The word says that straight and narrow is the path that leads to Him and broad and wide is the path that leads to destruction. 2012 is fast approaching and many will make New resolutions to lose weight, exercise, quit this and that. I personally will only resolve to draw closer to Christ, learn more of Him, and be a better servant for Christ.

How about YOU Fam, will you choose to love Him more? He won't twist your arm, He's a gentleman.

I'm jus sayin...Luv me.

***

Good morn. Fam..The body of Christ has to free itself from it's bloody issues so that it can reach the next generation.There is a generation of young people out there who are dying daily because we the body of Christ/the church, has so many issues that keep us bound, ineffective and out of God's perfect order.

In the following verses taken from Luke, Jesus could not deal with Jairus's daughter until He dealt with the woman with an issue of blood.
"So it was, when Jesus returned, that the multitude welcomed Him, for they were all waiting for Him. And behold, there came a man named Jairus, and he was a ruler of the synagogue. And he fell down at Jesus' feet and begged Him to come to his house, for he had an only daughter about twelve years of age, and she was dying.

But as He went, the multitudes thronged Him. Now a woman, having a flow of blood for twelve years, who had spent all her livelihood on physicians and could not be healed by any, came from behind and touched the border of His garment. And immediately her flow of blood stopped". Luke 8:40-44

In 2012 we must realize that twelve is the number of Apostolic Authority, government order. God is wanting to align His body, bringing it back into its rightful place in the realm of the earth.

It was not mere coincidence, that it was recorded in Luke the order in which Jesus worked on the earth. Today, God is wanting to deal with His Church(that's me and you). Realigning us and bringing us back into order. Only then can we be effective tools. Reaching not only the next generation, but the lost and misdirected who are being duped into believing that they can get

to God many ways.This week we will open this topic up and explore.
 I'm jus sayin.....Luv me.

***

Good morning Fam.. I have been touched by a situation that has caused me to take pause and reevaluate how we talk to people.

Maybe you too have seen or been in a situation where, if only someone had said the right thing, the situation would not have gotten out of hand.

Proverbs, which I call the book of wisdom, was written by King Solomon. Solomon, when asked by God to ask for anything he wanted, asked God for wisdom to rule His people wisely. In his writings Solomon instructs us on the use of the tongue.

Prov.15:1-2 "A soft answer turns away wrath, But a harsh word stirs up anger(wrath). The tongue of the wise uses knowledge rightly, But the mouth of fools pours forth foolishness".
 Wrath is defined as violent anger. Proverbs says that when we give a soft answer, even when we think the question was stupid, the answer was obvious or the person was slow (LOL), we turn away violent anger. Secondly, a harsh word (being critical, cynical, smart-mouthed, sharp-tongued or just plain hateful) stirs up the thing that most people would love to avoid, violent anger.

Husbands, wives, mothers, fathers, siblings, bosses, chosen and appointed leaders have spent countless hours, numerous dollars and countless resources paying for words spoken recklessly. Not to mention divorce courts and jails are filled with folks who did not take the time to weigh their words before speaking recklessly.

James 3:5-6(the Message) makes it plain. "It only takes a spark, remember, to set off a forest fire. A careless or wrongly placed word out of your mouth can do that. By our speech we can ruin the world, turn harmony to chaos, throw mud on a reputation, send the whole world up in smoke and go up in smoke with it, smoke right from the pit of hell."

I'm jus sayin....Luv me.

***

Good morn.FB Fam..Before taking a sidebar, we started this week speaking about the bloody issues the church must let go of so that we can reach a dying generation.

Isaiah 1:16-17 in the Message Bible says it better than I ever could, check it out.

"Quit your worship charades. I can't stand your trivial religious games: Monthly conferences, weekly Sabbaths, special meetings— meetings, meetings, meetings—I can't stand one more! Meetings for this, meetings for that. I hate them! You've worn me out! I'm sick of your religion, religion, religion, while you go right on sinning. When you put on your next prayer-performance, I'll be looking the other way. No matter how long or loud or often you pray, I'll not be listening. And do you know why? Because you've been tearing people to pieces, and your hands are bloody. Go home and wash up. Clean up your act. Sweep your lives clean of your evildoings so I don't have to look at them any longer. Say no to wrong. Learn to do good. Work for justice. Help the down-and-out. Stand up for the homeless. Go to bat for the defenseless."

Wow!Fam, who are we fooling when we only "play church".

I'm jus sayin....Luv me.

***

Good morn. Fam..So sorry that I was M.I.A on Friday, it seemed like I woke up with an elephant to eat and had to take it down one bite at a time.This New New Year has brought new challenges and I am sure that this is my year. The devil has been in attack mode with disruption after disruption. However, I choose to walk into the promises of God and will not let anything remove me from the path.

Many of us have made glowing declarations of new directions that we will endeavor to take up, walk in or pursue. I hope that so far you have been able to stick to your plans. Positive progress is admirable, especially when it's a step towards pleasing the Father. However, know this Fam...You can't put new wine in old wineskins, they will burst and the wine will be wasted.

Matt 9:17 "Nor do they put new wine into old wineskins, or else the wineskins break, the wine is spilled, and the wineskins are ruined. But they put new wine into new wineskins, and both are preserved."

It is absolutely imperative to renew the mind as you walk into new arenas. Many years have come and gone with New Year's resolutions broken and left unfulfilled. The main culprit in our breaking our vows of self-improvement is our unchanged, unrenewed minds.

Romans 12:2 "And do not be conformed to this world, but be transformed by the renewing of your mind, that you may prove what *is* that good and acceptable and perfect will of God."

A renewed mind equals a renewed life.

I'm jus sayin....Luv me.

***

Good morning Fam..Yesterday we parted on the note, "a renewed mind equals a renewed life". This is a principle that applies in the natural as well as the spiritual.

When I used to go into the "rooms"(N.A.- Narcotics Anonymous A.A.-Alcoholics Anonymous), one of the slogans that was so prevalent was, "you cannot receive different results by doing the same old things. If you always do what you always did, you'll always get what you always got".

God admonishes us in Romans 12:2 to be transformed by the renewing of our minds. God knows that most of our minds have been jacked up by what we call "stinkin thinkin" when we come to Him. It is not God's job to program us like a robot so that we automatically do everything correctly when we come to Him. It is assumed in some circles that we instantly become perfect when we are saved. LIES, I TELL YOU, LIES.

It is up to us to feed ourselves a steady diet of the Word of God, starting with the milk of the Word for babies in Christ. For the more mature Christian, the meat of the Word is necessary.

It is up to us to surround ourselves or fellowship with people that have and are willing to share their knowledge of the Word. Furthermore, it is totally up to us to put ourselves in a place of discipleship, desiring to be discipled in the things of God. We must allow the water of the Word to wash our minds of the muck of the world, and years of selfish ungodly worldly teaching.
 YES, FAM IT IS YOUR NEW MIND THAT WILL GIVE YOU A NEW YEAR.

You can declare all of the marvelous resolutions you want, but doing the same things will get you the same results.

I'm jus sayin....Luv me.

***

Good morning Fam..This week we have been discussing the New Year and how we make new grand resolutions for positive change. We've also established the fact that this can only happen as we renew our minds and walk in the newness of life.
 What I'm about to say may seem harsh to some.
For years I've seen churchgoers who have been systematic about their attending church, serving on this or that committee or choir, yet the've fruit produced in their lives has never changed. Millions claim Jesus, but have never made Him Lord. Their jobs, homes, image or their money is obviously their lord.
The Word says that you shall know a man by the fruit he produces. If the only fruit produced by a man is fruits of unrighteousness, who is he and even more important whose is he.

Romans 6:1-3(the Message) "So what do we do? Keep on sinning so God can keep on forgiving? I should hope not! If we've left the country where sin is sovereign, how can we still live in our old house there? Or didn't you realize we packed up and left there for good? That is what happened in baptism. When we went under the water, we left the old country of sin behind; when we came up out of the water, we entered into the new country of grace—a new life in a new land!

Fam don't get me wrong we will make mistakes(sin) until we leave this earth and our mortal bodies, but when Jesus is truly Lord and we have identified with Him in His death, burial and resurrection(baptism), we no longer plan sin, habitually commit sin or are ruled by sin.

I'm jus sayin.....Luv me.

Good morning Fam..Yesterday we shared Romans 6:1-3. Upon opening the Word this morning, the Message bible's translation of that same chapter through verse 14 spoke volumes to me, thus I'm sharing with you. Enjoy!

"That's what baptism into the life of Jesus means. When we are lowered into the water, it is like the burial of Jesus; when we are raised up out of the water, it is like the resurrection of Jesus. Each of us is raised into a light-filled world by our Father so that we can see where we're going in our new grace-sovereign country.

Could it be any clearer? Our old way of life was nailed to the cross with Christ, a decisive end to that sin-miserable life—no longer at sin's every beck and call! What we believe is this: If we get included in Christ's sin-conquering death, we also get included in his life-saving resurrection. We know that when Jesus was raised from the dead it was a signal of the end of death-as-the-end. Never again will death have the last word. When Jesus died, he took sin down with him, but alive he brings God down to us. From now on, think of it this way: Sin speaks a dead language that means nothing to you; God speaks your mother tongue, and you hang on every word. You are dead to sin and alive to God. That's what Jesus did.

That means you must not give sin a vote in the way you conduct your lives. Don't give it the time of day. Don't even run little errands that are connected with that old way of life. Throw yourselves wholeheartedly and full-time—remember, you've been raised from the dead!—into God's way of doing things. Sin can't tell you how to live. After all, you're not living under that old tyranny any longer. You're living in the freedom of God."

He's just sayin....Luv me.

***

"I will come down","this too shall pass","this won't last much longer","it's gonna wear off if I just hold on". These are the words I spoke when I had taken too much LSD(had a bad trip) or smoked too much PCP. These words kept me from running out into traffic or doing something else crazy to end it all.

Good morning Fam..Proverbs 6:2 "You are **snared by the words** of your mouth; You are taken **by the words** of your mouth".

This is a principle that works in the natural as well as the spiritual. I've put it to the test even in my ignorance, as I was way too high and in instances when others would have and did lose their very minds, doing the same things I was doing. God Kept Me, because of my words and of course His mercy and grace.

Now don't go and try what I did to see if it works, but be warned, be careful to watch your mouth.

Matt.12:37(NKJV)"For by your words you will be justified, and by your words you will be condemned."

(The Message)"Let me tell you something: Every one of these careless words is going to come back to haunt you. There will be a time of Reckoning. Words are powerful; take them seriously. Words can be your salvation. Words can also be your damnation."

Mark.11:23"For assuredly, I say to you, whoever says to this mountain, 'Be removed and be cast into the sea,' and does not doubt in his heart, but believes that those things he says will be done, he will have whatever he says."

You get what you say Fam!

I'm jus sayin.....Luv me.

***

Good morning Fam..Many of us go through "things", "situations", "problems" that we think could only happen to us. We feel we are unique and the only person to have ever faced the problem. It may seem to be an impassable wall that reaches from the ground you're standing on to the heavens.
Breaking out in a chorus of the song "nobody knows the trouble I've seen" would be appropriate for your situation in your present predicament. Your situation is exactly why God wrapped Himself in flesh and planted Himself in the womb of a virgin. He then lowered Himself to the place of being born in a barn, and walked this earth. He was tempted just as we are, yet without blowing it as we so often do.

Emmanuel (God with us) came and lived among us so that we would not have the excuse that God is asking us to do something that He was never subjected to.
 "Now that we know what we have—Jesus, this great High Priest with ready access to God—let's not let it slip through our fingers. We don't have a priest who is out of touch with our reality. He's been through weakness and testing, experienced it all—all but the sin. So let's walk right up to him and get what he is so ready to give. Take the mercy, accept the help". Hebrews 4:15-16 (The Message)

"No temptation has overtaken you except such as is common to man; but God is faithful, who will not allow you to be tempted beyond what you are able, but with the temptation will also make the way of escape, that you may be able to bear it."
1 Corinthians 10:13 (NKJV)

God knows what you are going through Fam.. You are not alone. Your situation is not new to Him, nor is it a surprise. Trust Him to handle it. He will!

"No test or temptation that comes your way is beyond the course of what others have had to face. All you need to remember is that God will never let you down; he'll never let you be pushed past

your limit; he'll always be there to help you come through it." 1Corinthians 10:13(The Message)

I'm jus sayin....Luv me.

***

Good morning Fam..Let's get real today!

Faith ain't faith until you are willing to step out of the boat, and into the water.

Who do you really trust? God or your feelings? God or your friends' opinions? God or your past experiences? God or the doctors report? God or the news media?

It is so easy to call yourself a Christian when all you have to do is put on your Sunday go to meeting clothes, your I'm blessed face and say all the right things when approached by other church-goers. However, does that make us Christians in word only, instead of Christians in deed? What happens in the middle of the week when we are faced with that challenge that seems insurmountable?

Do we trust Jesus when there seems to be no way out? Do we lean not to our own understanding by totally handing the problem over to Him? Or do we resort back to the way we knew to handle things, before we claimed to follow Him?

Come on Fam. it's 2012. We truly need to be honest about what it is that we trust, follow and believe in. There is no sin involved when we ask God to help our unbelief, but for us to front to others about our glowing faith, when we truly have none in tight places is a sin. In the streets we call it "perpetrating a fraud".

Peter displayed great faith when he stepped out of the boat to go and meet Jesus. His mistake, which is many of ours also, was when he took his eyes off of Jesus and focused on the waves. Is our focus on the waves, or is our focus on the one whom we confess, Jesus?

This is a self-examination moment, not time to worry about Sally or Sue but focus instead on YOU!

I'm jus sayin.....Luv me.

***

Good morning and TGIF Fam.."God is and He is a rewarder of those that diligently seek Him".

No matter what you go through, hell or high water, you must know that it is temporary. It won't last! What will last is God's love for you. Contrary to what we are taught sometimes, know this, God ain't mad at you, He's madly in love with YOU.

I'm gonna leave you with some meditations from the Message Bible that expound upon some of the things we have shared this week, Be Blessed!

"Consider it a sheer gift, friends, when tests and challenges come at you from all sides. You know that under pressure, your faith-life is forced into the open and shows its true colors. So don't try to get out of anything prematurely. Let it do its work so you become mature and well-developed, not deficient in any way". James 1:2-3 MSG

"So, we're not giving up. How could we? Even though on the outside it often looks like things are falling apart on us, on the inside, where God is making new life, not a day goes by without his unfolding grace. These hard times are small potatoes compared to the coming good times, the lavish celebration prepared for us. There's far more here than meets the eye. The things we see now are here today, gone tomorrow. But the things we can't see now will last forever". 2Cor.4:16-18 MSG

I'm jus sayin....Luv me.

***

Good morning Fam.."I DON'T CARE ANYMORE". As a matter of fact I will no longer spend my time worrying about things that God has promised me, He's got.
 Thanks to Dr Alan Bagg who broke this thing down like a shotgun yesterday. Let's go to the Word.

" I know what I'm doing. I have it all planned out—plans to take care of you, not abandon you, plans to give you the future you hope for." Jeremiah 29:11(Message)

"For I know the thoughts that I think toward you, says the LORD, thoughts of peace and not of evil, to give you a future and a hope."
Jeremiah 29:11(NKJV)

That is two different versions of the Bible. It's the same scripture and both versions tell us that our future is covered. God has thoughts of us, He has plans and His plans include giving me the future I hope for.

Good God, brother James Brown would say and I say GLORY TO GOD. This revelation frees me up to live. Because if someone has plans for a great future for you, and that same someone has all power. Why should I waste my time worrying about something that is already done?

One thing I know about God is, He is not a man that He should lie and He is bound to perform His Word.

We will go deeper in this teaching this week, but I gotta run.

I'm jus sayin......Luv me.

***

Good morning Fam.."I DON'T CARE"! Here we go again with another installation from my gleanings of Sunday's message.

Yesterday we covered Jeremiah 29:11. It spoke of the plans God has for us. Today we will go to the Amplified Bible.

"For we are God's [own] handiwork (His workmanship), recreated in Christ Jesus, [born anew] that we may do those good works which God predestined (planned beforehand) for us [taking paths which He prepared ahead of time], that we should walk in them [living the good life which He prearranged and made ready for us to live]. Ephesians 2:10

Today's word says expressly that we are God's handiwork. His workmanship born again to do the good works that He mapped out before the beginning of time. Living a good life which was prearranged. WOW!! That tells me that the way has already been prepared, all I need is the wisdom to walk in it.

GLORY TO GOD!!

My question to me(that's right,to me) is why have I spent so much time worrying about my future, when all I had to do is walk in it?

The Word in Matthew 6:34 says. "Therefore, do not worry about tomorrow, for tomorrow will worry about its own things. Sufficient for the day *is* its own trouble". Therefore, I will surmise that since He has a plan for my future, it's "all good", prearranged and mapped out. All I've got to do is walk in it. I would be stupid to worry, when all I have to do is have faith and trust His plan.

I feel like the commercial, "plop plop fizz fizz, oh, what a relief it is".

I'm jus sayin......Luv me.

***

Good morning. Fam..Yesterday I was asked by a reader of these posts if I was alright. The person had read the title "I don't care anymore" and thought that I had given up. For any of you who may have thought the same, know this. This series of messages is derived from a sermon I heard. It spoke of our sin of worrying about God's business,"US".

When we take it upon ourselves to worry about our futures, our kids, our anything. We are trying to take God's place. Worry is as the sin of pride and the Word says that pride goes before the fall.

If God says that He has got my life planned out, mapped out or charted, who am I to try and worry about tomorrow? All He wants is for me to trust His plan and walk in it.

No reader,I have not lost it. I am merely learning to be free and praying the same for you.

The following is a letter from the Message Bible that ties into that message,"I Don't Care".

God's Message:"Cursed is the strong one who depends on mere humans,Who thinks he can make it on muscle alone and sets God aside as dead weight.
He's like a tumbleweed on the prairie, out of touch with the good earth.
He lives rootless and aimless in a land where nothing grows.
"But blessed is the man who trusts me, God, the woman who sticks with God.
They're like trees replanted in Eden, putting down roots near the rivers—
Never a worry through the hottest of summers, never dropping a leaf, Serene and calm through droughts, bearing fresh fruit every season." Jeremiah 17:5-8(The Message Bible)

Cast your cares on The Father and don't take them back by worrying!

I'm jus sayin.....Luv me.

***

Good morning Fam.. All this week we have been sharing the theme, "I don't care". I really wanted to move on, but have been led to close this study with one last installation.

"I don't care" simply because I have been humbled and have conceded my rights to rule my life to God. Humility can be defined as casting your cares on God and letting Him be God. Many of us want to be God, you can tell it by our willingness to tell others how to live. By being frustrated when we ourselves have not reached a certain place that we think we ought to be in. Also by how instead of allowing God to direct our footsteps we try to be our own directors, as well as directing those in our circles.This behaviour has its roots in pride.

If you want to know how hard a pride fall can be, inbox me, been there done that and don't mind telling about it, cause it ain't pretty.

"Likewise, you younger people, submit yourselves to *your* elders. Yes, all of *you* be submissive to one another, and be clothed with humility, for "God resists the proud, But gives grace to the humble."
"Therefore, humble yourselves under the mighty hand of God, that He may exalt you in due time, casting all your care upon Him, for He cares for you."1Peter 5:5-7

Fam when we truly cast our cares on Him, Who redeemed you. You will give Him total authority, free reign, full rights to govern your life. We won't continually take those rights back by worrying, but we will trust Him to complete the job He has started.

Moreover, through hell and high water we will not allow our foot to be moved from the path He has started us on.

I'm jus sayin.....Luv me.

***

Good morning Fam..Blessings and peace to you, one and all.

My prayer today is that every eye reading this post is an eye that belongs to a person that is in a relationship with Jesus Christ. I don't mean, you go to a church. I don't mean yomamanem (your mama and them) pray for you. And I certainly didn't mean you've heard the Christmas story and felt all warm and fuzzy inside.

What I did mean is, that you have prayed the sinner's prayer and asked Jesus to come into your life. That there was a moment in time that you can remember when you stopped and said a certain prayer (the sinner's prayer) and you believed by faith that Jesus came into your life.

I am going to print such a prayer today and if you will speak it aloud with your mouth and believe it in your heart, you will be saved. You don't have to jump through any hoops, run down any aisle, nor will you have to be dunked, right hand fellowshipped or approved by any committee. The only requirement for it to work is that you speak it with your mouth, believe it in your heart and have the faith to accept the finished work of Christ. Here we go!

Dear Jesus, I come to You today admitting that I am a sinner. I also come believing that.You came to this earth, lived and died to pay for my sins and rose again on the third day just like You said You would. So I ask You today to forgive me of my sins. Come into my heart to live from this day forward. Speak to my spirit teaching me of your ways. Allow your Word to become living and alive in me, correcting my walk daily with You. I thank You for coming into my life today. I will listen for Your voice as You lead me in Your ways. IT'S IN JESUS'S NAME I PRAY. AMEN

Now if you just said that prayer and believed it by faith, "YOU ARE SAVED". You may not feel any different than you did before you prayed. Salvation has nothing to do with your feelings and everything to do with your faith in God, Who is His Word. If you have any questions like what to do next, inbox me. I'll be glad to help in any way I can.

I'm jus sayin......Luv me.

***

Good morning Fam.. Blessings and peace be unto you in the precious name of Jesus Christ. May His love run you down and take you over as you grow in the knowledge of Who He is and the magnificent love He has for you.

Fam., God ain't mad at you! Contrary to all of the religious jargon you have been taught. God has been portrayed as the mad punisher, sitting on a big old throne, with a big baseball bat, waiting for you to mess up. So that He can bust you in your head, peeling it back to the white meat. LOL
God's love is so deep for you that He clothed Himself in humanity, came to this sinful earth, became a human example of how we could live, healed our diseases, loved us where we were(even in our sin). Then He gave us the keys to life, took an awful beating for our sickness and submitted to dying a terrible death to become our perfect sacrifice for sin.

Fam, if that isn't love tell me what it is. Today, I just felt led to exhort and encourage you.

I'm jus sayin.......Luv me.

***

Good morning Fam..The Word of God says that we were "born in sin and shapen in iniquity". That is true because we are all born of the offspring of Adam the first man who introduced us to sin.

Each of us has a sin nature naturally. We don't have to be taught it.

Case in point, observe a baby, the most beautiful thing ever created. The baby comes to us as God's gift. They are all cute and cuddly, but dig this. Before we turn around, one of the first words out of their mouths is "NO". And it seems like as soon as they are able to walk they seem to know how to steal from the cookie jar and then deny it. Even with the cookie crumbs all around their cute little mouths. This is their Adamic nature, it comes naturally. No need to be taught.

Contrary to this is the nature we receive when Jesus comes into our lives, as we accept Him as our Lord and Saviour. We are naturally born in sin, and when we are "born-again" we are born into our new nature, or our Jesus nature.

Let's not get it twisted, contrary to what religion teaches, we are not perfect the moment we accept Jesus. Just as a baby in the natural world has to crawl, take a step at a time, sometimes stumbling, until they learn how to walk and ultimately run. We as baby Christians have to be raised to maturity. Matured to become the upstanding, righteous speaking, walking in blessing, children of the most high God.

It grieves God's heart when we claim Christ, are sincerely born-again and want to continue in our old lifestyles. Peer pressure, worrying about what your friends might think, fear of change. Lack of submission to discipleship and determination to do things our own way has caused many to miss out on the blessings that come with laying it all down at the feet of Jesus. Leaving it all there. While not looking back, realizing that your past is your past.

God wants to do a new thing in your life. His plans are for your ultimate good, yet many can't move forward for looking and going back to lifestyles that they know are not good for them.

"But Jesus said to him, "No one, having put his hand to the plow, and looking back, is fit for the kingdom of God."Luke 9:62(NKJV)

"Jesus said, "No procrastination. No backward looks. You can't put God's kingdom off till tomorrow. Seize the day."(The Message Bible)

Seize the day Fam., no looking back, moving ahead. God has so much more for you.

I'm just sayin......Luv me.

***

Good morning Fam..Glory to God for this marvelous weather we are experiencing! As far as I am concerned it can stay like this for the rest of the winter. lol
Now to the Word.

"And He said to them, "Go into all the world and preach the gospel to every creature. He who believes and is baptized will be saved; but he who does not believe will be condemned. And these signs will follow those who believe: In My name they will cast out demons; they will speak with new tongues; they will take up serpents; and if they drink anything deadly, it will by no means hurt them; they will lay hands on the sick, and they will recover". Mark 16:15-18

Fam it's the Word and I believe the whole Word, so let's not get spooked by it. Many of us feel like some parts of the bible were written only for folks that lived when it was written. I find it sad when I hear of preachers who discount parts of the Word as promises written only to generations past. I say "whoa" unto those preachers as I feel that they will have to answer to God for watering down His gospel.

Let us open up and digest as much of this scripture as time permits.

Go and preach the gospel, is simply saying, go and proclaim, tell about. You don't need an ordination, degree, title or any such thing to proclaim "the gospel". The gospel is defined as the good news of what Jesus has done for you. No one can tell your story like you.

Everyone cannot tell a story like mine of being delivered from a life of drug addiction, penal institutions, homelessness, rebelliousness, etcetera because the list goes on and on. That's my story, but what he has done for you, only you can tell.

I don't think that God has allowed any of us to go through the hell that we have endured so that we can sit on it. Somebody needs to hear how God brought you out, so that they too can have hope that there is a way out of what seems to them as an impossible situation.

"SO TELL IT FAM", it's the gospel.

The prophet Isaiah once said of the good news of what God had done for him, "it's like fire shut up in my bones and I just can't keep it to myself".

We're going to get more into this scripture tomorrow, stay tuned!

I'm jus sayin....Luv me.

***

Good morning and TGIF Fam..Wow the weekend is once again upon us. As I look out my window a beautiful day is taking shape. I am determined in my spirit to make this weekend and the rest of my days beautiful. I have received the revelation that it's all determined by what I think, what I allow to take up space in my mind.

The devil is not my problem, I AM. I AM the sum total of my thinking. I choose to not allow negative self deprecating thoughts that don't line up with the Word take up space in my mind. It's a choice FAM.

"For though we walk in the flesh, we do not war according to the flesh.For the weapons of our warfare *are* not carnal but mighty in God for pulling down strongholds,casting down arguments and every high thing that exalts itself against the knowledge of God, bringing every thought into captivity to the obedience of Christ." 2 Corinthians 10:3-5

"and the peace of God, which surpasses all understanding, will guard your hearts and minds through Christ Jesus.Finally, brethren, whatever things are true, whatever things *are* noble, whatever things *are* just, whatever things *are* pure, whatever things *are* lovely, whatever things *are* of good report, if *there is* any virtue and if *there is* anything praiseworthy—meditate on these things." Phillipians 4:7-8

Meditate, keep in mind, hold onto the thoughts of what God says about you. You are healed, you are blessed, you are whole, you are a royal priesthood, you are a child of the Most High God, you are prosperous. Bring into captivity and cast down negative thoughts, thoughts of lack, defeat, inadequacies, not enough, not good enough.

It is a choice that belongs to you alone.

I'm jus sayin.....Luv me.

***

Good morning Fam..This was one awesome weekend. I'm still high on the Spirit from the way God moved at church yesterday, it was something to behold and I'm glad I was there.

Today I'm preaching to myself. The following is a word that I need to get in my spirit and walk out. Should you find it helps you, be my guest using it.

"Go to the ant, you sluggard! Consider her ways and be wise,Which, having no captain, Overseer or ruler, Provides her supplies in the summer, *And* gathers her food in the harvest." Prov. 6:6-8

There is so much that the Lord wants to do for, in, and through me. Which would give Him the glory, that I have neglected by not moving fast enough. Procrastinating and shuffling my feet because of unbelief.

God wants to do things for me. I am sure many of those things won't be accomplished until I do my part. I know that there are promises of God for me that will require action from me to help the process. I need that pitbull tenacity or the persistence of the ant spoken of in Proverbs to accomplish some things.

Don't get me wrong. God doesn't need my help to be God. However, sometimes if we really want something bad enough we can't wait on Him to just drop it from heaven.

"Faith without works is dead."

I'm jus sayin......Luv me.

***

Good morning Fam.. Blessings and peace be unto you on this glorious day. You may look out of your window and wonder. What is he talking about? It's cloudy and cold.

But know this, when I turned fifty life started changing and I became grateful for every day that I was allowed to see. I've been to too many funerals for people younger than me.

Today I would like to share something from The Message Bible. Enjoy!

Seven Things God Hates
Here are six things God hates, and one more that he loathes with a passion:
eyes that are arrogant, a tongue that lies, hands that murder the innocent,
a heart that hatches evil plots, feet that race down a wicked track,
a mouth that lies under oath, a troublemaker in the family.
Warning on Adultery

Good friend, follow your father's good advice; don't wander off from your mother's teachings.Wrap yourself in them from head to foot; wear them like a scarf around your neck.
Wherever you walk, they'll guide you; whenever you rest, they'll guard you; when you wake up, they'll tell you what's next.
For sound advice is a beacon, good teaching is a light, moral discipline is a life path.
They'll protect you from wanton women, from the seductive talk of some temptress.
Don't lustfully fantasize on her beauty, nor be taken in by her bedroom eyes.
You can buy an hour with a whore for a loaf of bread, but a wanton woman may well eat you alive.

Can you build a fire in your lap and not burn your pants?
Can you walk barefoot on hot coals and not get blisters?
It's the same when you have sex with your neighbor's wife: Touch
her and you'll pay for it. No excuses.
Hunger is no excuse for a thief to steal; When he's caught he has to
pay it back, even if he has to put his whole house in hock.
Adultery is a brainless act, soul-destroying, self-destructive;
Expect a bloody nose, a black eye, and a reputation ruined for
good.
For jealousy detonates rage in a cheated husband; wild for
revenge, he won't make allowances. Nothing you say or pay will
make it all right; neither bribes nor reason will satisfy him."
Proverbs 6:16-35

He's jus sayin.....Luv me.

***

Good morning Fam..This morning I'm at the hospital in Richmond
with my beautiful wife. Upon opening the Word this morning the
Lord spoke these words to my spirit. Just thought I'd share them
with you. Trust God, not your circumstances.

"Thus, says the Lord, the King of Israel, And his Redeemer, the
Lord of hosts:
'I *am* the First and I *am* the Last; Besides Me *there is* no God.
And who can proclaim as I do?
Then let him declare it and set it in order for Me,
Since I appointed the ancient people.
And the things that are coming and shall come,
Let them show these to them.
Do not fear, nor be afraid;
Have I not told you from that time, and declared *it?*
You *are* My witnesses.
Is there a God besides Me?

Indeed, *there is* no other Rock;
I know not *one.*'"
Isaiah 44:6-8

Fam. He's Alpha and Omega. There is no other Rock, no other God like our God. We are totally trusting God, and all is well.

If you or anyone you know is going through sickness, doctor visits, endless procedures and have received a negative report. Know that there is no other Rock, but Jesus. As for me and my house we will serve and trust the Lord.

I'm jus sayin….Luv me.

***

Good morning Fam.. Happy Valentine's Day!

On this day every year many make their declarations of love. Many buy beautiful cards, chocolates, go out on fabulous intimate dates and buy out the flower shops to declare their love one to another. Sometimes this one day is the only day that many will say the words, I LOVE YOU to their significant other, sad but true. On the other hand, is those of us who don't mind speaking the words, yet we don't have a clue what this word LOVE means. First Corinthians chapter 13 breaks down the meaning of love to its lowest common denominator. I would love for you to go over the entire chapter, but for the sake of time I will go over the portions that pertain to the love we claim for our significant other on Valentines day.

*Love suffers long (Do we actually put up with suffering because we love someone and are willing to suffer to be with them or do we quit and walk away?)

* *and* is kind;(Are we prone to be kind even when we disagree, when we really want to give that person a piece of our mind?)
*love does not envy;(Are you actually joyful when that person is promoted, prospered or exalted and you didn't have anything to do with it?);
* love does not parade itself (love does not seek out it's own agenda pushing "what I want", "how great I am","look at me")
*is not puffed up (is not proud and boastful, bragging on "the merits of me");
*does not behave rudely (is not brash, harsh, mean-natured),
* does not seek its own (knows that it's not about me),
*is not provoked (is not easily pushed off it's square, intimidated into acting out of character, pushed to act ugly),
*thinks no evil(no matter what is said about your significant other, if it is evil you won't believe it unless it's confirmed by them) ;
*does not rejoice in iniquity(does not rejoice in willful, intended sin committed by the significant other, but desires positive change for their good),
*but rejoices in the truth (is happy for manifestations of truth);
*bears all things(puts up with whatever, while praying and hoping for the best),
*believes all things (believes for the best),
*hopes all things (hopes for the best),
*endures all things (endures hell and high water to be together).

Now Fam, ask yourselves, do I really love?

I'm jus sayin......Luv me

***

Good morning FB Fam.. Man with all the love proclamations I heard yesterday, I pondered about the love Jesus has for us. I wondered if in fact, any of us had the capacity to love as He loved.

Check this out.

"Greater love has no one than this, than to lay down one's life for his friends." John 15:**13**

"In this is love, not that we loved God, but that He loved us and sent His Son *to be* the propitiation for our sins."**1 John 4:10**

Fam, yesterday I heard a lot of love declarations. Many spoke of their love for their significant others on Valentine's day. However the scriptures speak of a love so strong that it would.
*lay down it's life,
*willfully subject itself to a horrible death,
*take a beating that was beyond human comprehension
*to demonstrate that love.

Maybe this is a stupid question, but I'm gonna ask it anyway. How many of you would subject yourselves to the kind of beating Jesus took to prove your love for your significant other, your child or your mom and dad?

How many of you would give your only child to pay for a debt owed by another to show your love for them?

I would be inclined to answer these questions for the majority and that answer would be, no we could not do it. I might think that I could, but after the first two lashes of the whip, I know that I would be begging for another way out, another way to demonstrate my love.

Fam, food for thought: From now on when we declare our love for one another, visualize the price Jesus paid to demonstrate His love. Take pause to thank Him and give Him the glory for His marvelous gift that was demonstrated in blood.

I'm jus sayin.....Luv me.

***

Good morning Fam..Please excuse my tardiness, I'm off so I slept in. LOL

Today I would like to touch on a very touchy subject. I say touchy because we have been taught for years, even from pulpits, that the devil is all that. Many believe we should fear him and his works. He wants us to believe that he is an adversary worthy of our respect. LIES!!!
Fam he is a defeated foe. He's been defeated since Jesus died on the cross, descended into hell and snatched the KEYS to hell and the grave from him.

The Bible says that the devil walks about like a roaring lion, seeking whom he may devour. "Like a roaring lion."

Here's the profile of the roaring lion. I learned it from the National Geographic Channel.

The roaring lion is the old lion without any teeth. He is deteriorating in health and really not a threat. His job is to roar to scare the prey into the jaws of the young strong lions who can do some damage. When a lion that can kill is approaching, you won't hear a thing. He won't warn you. The roaring lion can't hurt you. The devil is a defeated foe. Our big Brother, Jesus, has guaranteed us the win.

I once heard a sermon by Jesse Duplantis that opened my eyes to who my greatest adversary really was, IT'S ME. My flesh is my biggest enemy. When I have not fed my Spirit man through the reading of the Word, worship and fellowship with others walking in Christ, I may do anything. It's my flesh that leads me to desire things contrary to what is God's desire for me. I submit to you today that your flesh is your greatest adversary also.

"For though we walk in the flesh, we do not war according to the flesh. For the weapons of our warfare *are* not carnal but mighty in God for pulling down strongholds, casting down arguments and every high thing that exalts itself against the knowledge of God, bringing every thought into captivity to the obedience of Christ, and being ready to punish all disobedience when your obedience is fulfilled." 2 Cor. 10:3-6
"So then, those who are in the **flesh** cannot please God".
<u>Romans 8:8</u>
"For if you live according to the **flesh** you will die; but if by the Spirit you put to death the deeds of the body, you will live."
Romans 8:13
I'm jus sayin…..Luv me.

***

Good morning and TGIF Fam..What a beautiful day we have to start off the weekend. I've been reading posts from folks who are going through a struggle right now. I've given out what I've been given so that we may use it to expedite our breakthrough.
The truth of the matter is, the Word says, in the end WE WIN.
It is only a matter of holding on to your faith and speaking what you desire (creating your future with your words) until you see what you hope for. However, my words, as effective as they are to some, is nothing like The WORD.

I would like to leave you this week with some Word from The Message Bible that speaks to all of us in the struggle.
"So, what do you think? With God on our side like this, how can we lose? If God didn't hesitate to put everything on the line for us, embracing our condition and exposing himself to the worst by sending his own Son, is there anything else he wouldn't gladly and freely do for us? And who would dare tangle with God by messing with one of God's chosen? Who would dare even to point a finger? The One who died for us—who was raised to life for us!—is in the presence of God at this very moment sticking up for us. Do you think anyone is going to be able to drive a wedge between us and Christ's love for us? There is no way! Not trouble, not hard times, not hatred, not hunger, not homelessness, not bullying threats, not backstabbing, not even the worst sins listed in Scripture:"
"They kill us in cold blood because they hate you.
We're sitting ducks; they pick us off one by one.
None of this fazes us because Jesus loves us. I'm absolutely convinced that nothing—nothing living or dead, angelic or demonic, today or tomorrow, high or low, thinkable or unthinkable—absolutely nothing can get between us and God's love because of the way that Jesus our Master has embraced us."
Rom.8:31-39

Have a blessed weekend Fam. Find, get with, and seek out others to join with in offering God some corporate praise, there is power in agreement.

I'm jus sayin........Luv me.***
Good morning Fam..The Church (you,the believer is the church, not a building) has been charged and indicted(enough evidence has been collected to send this to trial in the high court). For the crime of reckless mouthing(putting your mouths on other believers recklessly), being judgemental (judging when you had

no right to do so), possessing a self-righteous spirit(when the bible says that our righteousness is as filthy rags) and harboring religion(ignoring relationship with Christ while holding onto the traditions of men.) Thinking that your works will get you into heaven. Browbeating those you think are not as good as you. And finally, ignoring the gospel of grace (neglecting the word of God).

You are now being advised to secure an attorney to defend you for your trial by jury (the chief counselor, Jesus, has been recommended for your defense).

To reach Him just drop to your knees and repent (have a godly sorrow for your transgressions and make an abrupt turnaround away from them and to Him) He will always answer your call and He is undefeated in court.

I'm jus sayin.....Luv me.

About the Author

Don Brown comes from Fredericksburg, VA, a small town that sits midway between Washington DC and Richmond, Virginia.

He grew up attending one of the "big three" Baptist churches there, and participated in its programs from the usher board, to the choirs, and reading of scriptures, when called upon to participate.

Outside of church he took advantage of recreation department sponsored programs such as archery, marksmanship, karate classes and swimming.

Blessed with a powerful singing voice, Don has been performing since kindergarten. While his music is steeped in the tradition of soul artists like Otis Redding, and the Temptations, Don's true musical inspiration comes from the years spent singing in church choirs and acting as a church worship leader.

Don also was an integral part of the theater groups "Shades of Soul" and "Harambee", where he developed acting skills which led to parts in college level productions at Mary Washington College, now The University of Mary Washington.

Don was also exposed to street life/hustling at an early age. Money was tight in his home, so he learned to hustle "nickel bags", LSD and other pills that were in demand from people frequenting the local bar, sitting around the corner from his childhood home.

After high school Don went to live in the nation's capital, and soon found salvation, making Jesus the Lord and Savior of his life. He became involved with spirit filled churches that taught the bible intensely, practiced fasting, much prayer, and healing by the laying on of hands.

For six years Don absorbed the Word, but was drawn away by his fleshly inclinations for sex and drugs. Besieged by guilt and shame he backslid out of the church and into the streets, where he drove gypsy cabs at nights, and participated in all that the underbelly of the city had to offer.

Soon he was homeless, strung out on heroin and PCP. That life led him to a cycle of incarcerations. He gives the glory to God for protection in those places which were never pretty and far from rehabilitative.

Don's last tour of the penal system was after his first wife, Lisa's passing. They met as he was evangelizing in the Bronx, New York with God's Miracles, a singing group outreach from New Life For Youth, a Christian Rehabilitation organization.

When Lisa passed Don became mad at God. He returned to his old drug lifestyle, secretly on a suicide mission. Suffering from the guilt of the way he handled her last year, he hoped to overdose and join her. Don always says that he was never arrested, only rescued. It seemed as if the only way God could get to him was to lock him up, away from the streets.

Don has been truly tested by fire. Glory to God, his savior never gave up on him. Today his life is a testament to what God can bring anyone through.

The pages of this book boast of the goodness of God and His never ending love for all of us!

Made in the USA
Middletown, DE
31 January 2024

48759025R00099